Norwegian Baking

Nevada Berg

Norwegian Baking

THROUGH THE SEASONS

90 Sweet and Savory Recipes from *North* WILD KITCHEN

PRESTEL

Munich · London · New York

Contents

Some days you just need to bake.
Whatever the occasion, whatever the sky.

Introduction

Baking provides a wide canopy of experiences. It can be simple and complex, beautiful and imperfect, time consuming and swift. It's creation by our hands, the marriage of ingredients, a thoughtful journey, a way of celebrating, a way of building on the relationships around us, a gesture of love. It's our past, our present, and our future—telling the stories of what has been, making memories in the moment, and creating something to be carried into tomorrow.

When thinking about what kind of cookbook would follow my first, *North Wild Kitchen: Home Cooking from the Heart of Norway*, I always knew deep down it would have to be about baking. The smells of butter melting and cardamom drifting in the air, bowls of custard cooling on the counter, seeds strewn across the plate, bubbles forming on flatbread over the hot griddle, flour everywhere—these are the commonplace moments found in my kitchen in Norway. The treats and delectable breads that bring so much joy, sustenance, and warmth throughout the year are just too good and too many not to give them the space they need to be shared and enjoyed.

My first baked good in Norway was a *skillingsbolle* ("cinnamon bun"). Swirls of dough laced with cinnamon sugar became a tradition I always indulged in whenever I visited my husband's family home of Bergen, where skillingsboller hail from. It was the beginning of a joyous journey filled with cakes, creams, breads, pastries, porridges, crackers, and everything in between. Each holiday, celebration, visit to a friend's home or local *bakeri*—"bakery"—opened my eyes to the wonders of Norwegian baking, with its deeply rooted traditions and newer influences. I've spent the last few years looking through cookbooks, old and new, their pages filled with exciting and interesting recipes. Some recipes are still popular today, some are forgotten, some are a bit more unusual, and some, perhaps, are better left as ink on the page. I've taken what I've gathered, along with my experiences and travels

around this breathtaking country and my own creations, to put together this collection of recipes for you. They tell so many stories and are often shaped by the unfolding seasons.

On paper, Norway has four seasons, but with the way the light moves in the north and the way nature follows, it feels more appropriate to refer to five seasons. Mirrored in the chapters, you'll find how we take our baking cues from the evolution of the seasons. After the winter solstice (the darkest time of the year), the start of the new year brings lighter days and yet still a lingering darkness. This is *vinterlys*—"winter light." When snow still remains, but the days seem longer and buds, at long last, start popping, it's spring's *nytt lys*—"new light." Summer is marked by the longest day of the year, as the *midnattssol*—"midnight sun"—shines bright. Where once the days were bright and long, the sky soon burns with a fire of red, purple, orange, and pink tones and the air turns both chilly and warm, like *ild og is*—"fire and ice." And as autumn passes the baton to winter, the days grow shorter and dark. This is *mørketid*—the "dark time."

Each season ushers in its own ingredients and occasions, carving out a path to help guide us in our kitchens. One thing you learn quickly when living in Norway, is that your home extends beyond its walls. Your time is shared both under a roof and in the open expanse of the surrounding landscape. Not even bad weather can, nor should, contain an individual to an enclosed space. That's why every opportunity to explore the outdoors is relished upon and why nature plays such an important role in the kitchen, whether you're anticipating new buds in spring, waiting for the berries to pop in summer, gathering a bounty of ingredients at harvest, or using preserves and spices in winter. Whatever the seasons bring, I hope you will allow them to guide you in creating your own baking story. I also hope you will feel the warmth of the Norwegian kitchen wherever you are.

Notes on Equipment and Ingredients

Baking should make you feel empowered and allow for your creativity and intuition to shine. I would never wish for anyone to feel limited or helpless in the kitchen simply because they don't have specific equipment or ingredients. While necessary in some instances, they shouldn't deter you from the joy of making something you want to create. I have provided a list of equipment and ingredients that are good to have, but there are almost always substitutions you can use in place of them.

EQUIPMENT

Brush—I like to use a designated hand broom/dust brush when cooking over the *takke*. It's a helpful tool to brush away any excess flour that might start burning on the dry griddle.

Kransekake Rings—These are available to buy in specialty shops and online and are used for making *kransekake*, an almond wreath cake. If you can't find the rings, you can always stencil the shapes by hand or make simple cookies with the dough.

Krumkake Iron—This highly embellished iron is used to make *krumkaker* and *strull*, "wafer cookies." Look for these at specialty shops and online.

Lefse Stick—This long and thin wooden stick is used for transferring *lefse* and flatbreads to the griddle and for turning them while cooking. It's a great tool to have if you plan on making lefse or flatbreads often. As an alternative, use the handle end of a long wooden spoon or spatula, or an unused wooden paint stirring stick.

Ricer—This tool is very helpful for getting a smooth consistency from the cooked potatoes used to make recipes like *lomper* and potato tarts. If you plan on baking Norwegian goods often, I highly recommend investing in one; otherwise, use a good potato masher.

Rolling Pins—In Norway, there are various types of indented rolling pins to make lefse and flatbreads. You can use a regular rolling pin for all of these recipes.

Scale—I include both imperial and metric measurements, but I highly recommend weighing ingredients with a scale, as it is much more accurate. In some instances, the conversions are rounded slightly up or down to match more closely with the other and make it easier for you, independent of which measurement system you use. These slight differences should not affect the outcome of the recipes.

Stand Mixer—This is a true friend in the kitchen, as a good one will save you effort and time. So many people have stand mixers these days that many of the recipes call for using one. However, you can always use your hands to knead, or opt for electric beaters, a hand whisk, or a wooden spoon for mixing.

Takke—I adore my takke. This Norwegian griddle is round, very large, and can be electric or heated by fire. If you can't access one, use a frying pan instead. You won't be able to cook as many cakes or breads at once, or make them as large, but they'll turn out great, nonetheless.

Waffle Iron—The Norwegian waffle iron is imprinted with a heart design, giving waffles that distinctive look. However, you can always use a normal waffle iron.

INGREDIENTS

Butter—Common Norwegian butter tends to be lightly salted and I use this butter in all my baking and cooking. Room temperature butter should be soft and malleable but keep its shape.

Brown Cheese (Brunost)—This iconic Norwegian cheese is actually a by-product of cheesemaking, when leftover whey is cooked down until it caramelizes and turns a lovely deep brown color. Look for the international brand, Ski Queen® Classic, which can be found in specialty shops and online.

Cultured Milk—I use *kulturmelk* and *kefir*, two soured milk products, in both cheese making and baking. For the recipes in this book when I normally use kulturmelk, I have listed buttermilk in the ingredient list. For the recipes using kefir, it's also fine to substitute buttermilk.

Dairy—Norwegian dairy products contain high percentages of fat. All cream must be heavy cream and contain about 36 percent fat. I specify which recipes require full-fat dairy products; elsewhere you can use lower fat products.

Eggs—I use locally sourced eggs and always leave them at room temperature, unless it's really hot and then I put them in the fridge and take out what I need an hour or so before use. Use room temperature eggs for these recipes. Also, many recipes call for either yolks or whites. I store leftover whites in the refrigerator to use within three days; they are great for making meringue. Leftover yolks tend not to store as well, so I prefer using them as soon as possible in custards or other recipes.

Flour—Some recipes call for strong white bread flour, which is the same as bread flour, strong white flour, and strong flour and has a higher protein content than all-purpose. If you don't have strong white bread flour, substitute with all-purpose flour, also known as plain flour. Some recipes call for whole flours, such as whole wheat or whole rye, where the whole kernel—the bran, germ, and endosperm—are ground into a fine flour, making a coarser and more nutritious product. For rye flour, I sometimes use light rye flour (also known as white rye flour). For spelt flour, I sometimes use white spelt flour. For einkorn and emmer, I use fine stone-ground flours. Again, for more accuracy, I highly recommend using a scale to weigh flour.

Fruits and Berries—Many of the fruits and berries we use are grown in our garden or picked in the wild. Here are substitutions for those that might be harder to access:
· Bilberries (European blueberries)—blueberries
· Black currants—blackberries (although, they do have different taste profiles)

· Cloudberries—golden raspberries or even red raspberries for an alternative
· Lingonberries—cranberries
· Wild strawberries—strawberries

Lukewarm Water/Milk—When referring to lukewarm water or milk, it should be the same as body temperature, which is 98.6°F (37°C).

Oil—I use good quality rapeseed oil (also known as canola oil) in most of my cooking and baking. In all the recipes calling for oil, I suggest using a mild-flavored oil like canola oil or a mild olive oil.

Salt—I mostly use table salt, but I also occasionally use sea salt for finishing.

Spices—A potent spice will bring so much life to a recipe. As spices have a short shelf life, keep smaller amounts on hand and update as needed.

Sugar—I always use granulated sugar unless specified in the recipe. Some recipes call for pearl sugar, which is a more coarse, decorative sugar that keeps its shape when baking. Look for Scandinavian varieties.

Syrup—In Norway, there are two kinds of syrup, light and dark. Both are types of inverted sugar syrups. The closet substitute for light syrup is golden syrup, which you should be able to find in specialty shops. For dark syrup, substitute with light molasses.

Vanilla—For certain recipes, I prefer to use vanilla beans, but a high-quality pure vanilla extract—not essence—is a good substitute.

Yeast—Fresh yeast is readily available and typically used in Norwegian baking, however, to make it easier, my recipes use instant yeast. It does not require activation, making it a good alternative in baking. If using fresh yeast, make sure to dissolve it in the liquid before adding it to the recipe. I do use active dry yeast when making pizza dough, as I am used to preparing it in this manner, but it does require activation.

Winter Light

❖ Vinterlys

❖ **DARKNESS HAS BEGUN** its slow retreat here in the North, as the new year arrives off the heels of the darkest day of the year, the winter solstice. The days are short but regaining strength with each new morning. This is the time when winter shows its other side—a balance to the dark—the light.

The sky is a frosted blue or heavy grey, which at times breaks into strokes of pastels and vibrant hues as the sun rises and sets. The earth is laden with snow and the cold can be bitter, but the sun's rays provide glimmers of warmth on icy cheeks. Time is spent baking more wholesome breads and flatbreads following the treat-laden holiday times of *mørketid*. It's a fresh start, a chance to warm the kitchen and the soul at the same time.

February brings *Fastelavn* (Carnival) celebrations, with indulgent treats like cream-filled buns. As March enters, we nestle ourselves in the mountains for as many ski runs as we can fit in and time spent warming ourselves by the fire with a baked good in one hand and a warm drink in the other. It's a time to fill our bellies with good things as we look forward to the coming of spring.

Sun Buns

In parts of northern Norway, to mark the return of the sun after the dark time (*mørketiden*), these *solboller*, or "sun buns," also known as *solskinsboller*, or "sunshine buns," are often enjoyed. Egg custard with its yellow hue sits front and center surrounded by sweet dough as a palpable symbol of the sun. Some variations sit the custard atop a plain bun, while others, including mine, place it on a cinnamon bun. It's a very sweet way of welcoming in the lighter days.

Makes 12 buns

❖ **FOR THE BUNS**

1¼ cups (300 ml) whole milk

4 cups plus 2 tablespoons (500 g) all-purpose flour, sifted

6 tablespoons (75 g) granulated sugar

2 teaspoons (¼ ounce / 7 g) instant yeast

1½ teaspoons ground cardamom

¼ teaspoon salt

2 large eggs, at room temperature

⅓ cup (75 g) lightly salted butter, cut into small pieces

❖ **FOR THE FILLING**

4 tablespoons (56 g) lightly salted butter, at room temperature

2 tablespoons granulated sugar

1 tablespoon ground cinnamon

❖ **FOR THE CUSTARD**

2 large egg yolks, at room temperature

⅓ cup (65) granulated sugar

2 tablespoons cornstarch

2 cups (480 ml) whole milk

½ vanilla bean, split lengthwise, or 1 teaspoon vanilla extract

For the buns, in a small saucepan, heat the milk over low heat until lukewarm.

In a stand mixer fitted with the dough hook attachment, combine the flour, sugar, yeast, cardamom, and salt. Add the lukewarm milk and 1 of the eggs. Knead on low for 8 minutes. Add the butter and knead on medium for about 5 minutes more, or until the dough is very elastic and somewhat moist. Transfer the dough to a lightly buttered bowl, cover with a tea towel, and let rise in a warm spot for about 1 hour, or until doubled in size.

For the filling, in a small bowl, combine the butter, sugar, and cinnamon.

Once the dough has doubled in size, line 2 baking sheets with parchment paper.

On a lightly floured surface, using a rolling pin and more flour as needed to prevent sticking, roll out the dough into a large rectangle that measures roughly 20 x 15 inches (50 x 38 cm). Spread the filling evenly across the dough all the way to the edges. Starting on 1 of the long sides, roll the dough around the filling to form a long, roughly 20 inch (50 cm), log. Using a sharp knife, cut the log crosswise into 12 equal size buns. Divide the buns between the prepared baking sheets, cover with a tea towel, and let rise in a warm spot for 40 minutes.

For the custard, in a large bowl, whisk together the egg yolks and sugar then whisk in the cornstarch.

Put the milk in a small saucepan. Scrape the seeds from the vanilla bean into the milk and add the scraped bean (or add the vanilla extract). Place over low heat and warm until just about to simmer. Remove the vanilla bean, then gradually pour the warm milk in a slow, steady stream into the egg yolk and sugar mixture, whisking constantly to avoid curdling the eggs. →

Pour the mixture back into the saucepan and cook over medium heat for 5 to 8 minutes, or until the custard has thickened considerably. Remove from the heat and let cool slightly.

Preheat the oven to 400°F (200°C).

Using your fingers or the back of spoon, make a large indentation in the center of each bun, then fill with 2 to 3 tablespoons of the prepared custard.

In a small bowl, whisk the remaining egg and lightly brush it on top of the dough. Bake for about 10 minutes, or until nicely browned. Transfer to a wire rack to cool before serving. Store at room temperature in an airtight container for up to 2 days.

No-Knead Emmer and Spelt Bread

A good, hearty loaf that can stand up to its toppings and leave you satisfied is always welcome in our house. That's what I like about this emmer and spelt bread. It's also nutritious and you can mix everything together the night before and bake it in the morning to enjoy for a late breakfast or lunch. Emmer, like einkorn, is an ancient heirloom grain, considered one of the earliest forms of cultivated grains, and is grown organically in Norway. It's high in protein and low in gluten with lovely nutty notes. I like to combine it with spelt flour for a lighter loaf, as it can be quite dense on its own. This recipe yields one large loaf, but you can always double it and freeze a loaf for later. Serve with your favorite toppings.

Makes 1 loaf

4 cups plus 2 tablespoons (500 g) white spelt flour

1½ cups plus 2 tablespoons (195 g) stone-ground emmer flour

1½ teaspoons salt

1 teaspoon (⅛ ounce / 3.5 g) instant yeast

5 tablespoons (50 g) flax seeds

5 tablespoons (50 g) sesame seeds

2½ cups (600 ml) cold water

In a large bowl, whisk together the spelt flour, emmer flour, salt, yeast, flax seeds, and sesame seeds. Pour in the cold water and stir to form a dough. Cover with a tea towel and let rise in a warm spot overnight (12 to 18 hours).

Butter a 9 x 5 inch (23 x 13 cm) loaf pan.

After 12 to 18 hours, on a lightly floured surface, knead the dough 3 to 4 times, then shape into a rectangle and place in the prepared loaf pan. Cover with a tea towel and let rise in a warm spot for about 1 hour, or until doubled in size.

Once the dough has doubled in size, preheat the oven to 425°F (220°C).

Take a second loaf pan, the same size as the first, and arrange it, upside down, on top of the filled loaf pan to create a tent and cover the dough. This will help create steam while the bread is baking, giving it a nice crust. Alternatively, you can tent foil over the top, leaving enough space for the dough to rise while baking without touching the foil. Bake for 40 minutes, then remove the loaf pan or foil on top and bake for about 20 minutes more, or until golden brown.

Let the bread rest in the loaf pan for 10 minutes before transferring to a wire rack to cool completely. Store at room temperature in an airtight bag for up to 2 days.

Rustic Einkorn and Herb Bread

Einkorn is an ancient grain that now has a permanent place in my household. It's typically richer in antioxidants and beta carotene than modern wheat varieties and has a complex taste. In this recipe, herbs balance the einkorn flour and you get a remarkable and tasty bread with a distinct and flavorful aroma that is a welcome change from everyday loaves. You can use fresh herbs or dried, as I have here—we preserve them from the garden. If using fresh, just double the amounts. Any leftover bread can be put to good use as croutons or in savory bread puddings for brunch.

Makes 1 loaf

4 cups plus 2 tablespoons (500 g) stone-ground einkorn flour

1 teaspoon (⅛ ounce / 3.5 g) instant yeast

1 teaspoon salt

2 teaspoons dried parsley

2 teaspoons dried thyme

1 teaspoon dried rosemary, dill, or chives

1½ cups (360 ml) warm water

In a stand mixer fitted with the dough hook attachment, combine the flour, yeast, salt, parsley, thyme, and rosemary. Pour in the warm water and knead on medium for about 5 minutes, or until the dough is smooth and workable. Transfer to an oiled bowl, cover with a tea towel, and let rise in a warm spot for about 1 hour, or until doubled in size. I find that in colder months, I need to let the dough rise for up to 2 hours.

Once the dough has doubled in size, preheat the oven to 400°F (200°C). Place a cast-iron pan on a bottom rack of the oven, beneath the middle rack where the bread will bake. Line a baking sheet with parchment paper.

On a lightly floured surface, gently knead the dough, while folding over the edges to bring it together and form an oval shape. Place the dough on the prepared baking sheet and dust the top with some flour. Use a sharp knife to make a long and shallow cut in the center of the top of the dough, then cover with a tea towel while the oven is heating.

When the oven is ready, place the bread on the middle shelf of the oven. Carefully and quickly, pour 1 cup (240 ml) of warm water in the cast-iron pan and immediately close the oven door to create steam for a nice crust. Bake for 30 to 35 minutes, or until golden brown.

Let the bread cool for 10 minutes, then transfer to a wire rack and let cool for 1 hour before cutting into it. Store at room temperature in an airtight bag for up to 2 days.

Einkorn and Honey Rolls

If you're new to using einkorn flour, this is a wonderful starter recipe. I really enjoy the nutty and toasty notes from the einkorn, and the addition of honey gives it a slightly sweet taste. You can also use this recipe to make a small loaf by placing the dough in a loaf pan for the second rise and baking for 35 minutes. Serve with your favorite toppings.

Makes 8 rolls

3 cups (360 g) stone-ground einkorn flour

1 teaspoon (⅛ ounce / 3.5 g) instant yeast

1 teaspoon salt

2 tablespoons runny honey

1 cup plus 2 teaspoons (250 ml) warm water

½ tablespoon mild-flavored oil

In the bowl of a stand mixer fitted with the dough hook attachment, combine the flour, yeast, and salt.

Stir the honey into the warm water to combine, then pour into the stand mixer, followed by the oil, and knead on low for about 5 minutes, or until the dough is somewhat wet and sticky. Transfer the dough to a lightly oiled bowl, cover with a tea towel, and let rise in a warm spot for about 1 hour, or until doubled in size.

Once the dough has doubled in size, line a baking sheet with parchment paper. Divide the dough into 8 equal pieces and shape into balls. Place the balls of dough on the prepared baking sheet, cover with a tea towel, and let rise in a warm spot for 1 hour.

Preheat the oven to 350°F (180°C). If desired, use a sharp knife to make shallow cuts in a cross design on the tops of the balls of dough. Bake for about 20 minutes, or until golden.

Let the rolls cool slightly before serving. Store at room temperature in an airtight bag for up to 2 days.

Crusty Rolls

Rolls are a dietary staple in the Nordic kitchen. Unassuming but indispensable, they are the foundation to be built upon for a hearty breakfast or lunch, mostly during the weekends when the first meal is a leisurely one. While *rundstykker* are available everywhere in Norway, I tend to favor the homemade variation, as they're delicious, easy to make, and you can use whichever flours, seeds, and nuts you have on hand. Cut these crusty beauties horizontally in half and serve with your favorite toppings.

Makes 10 rolls

¾ cup plus 1 tablespoon (200 ml) milk

2¼ cups (270 g) strong white bread flour

1¼ cups (150 g) whole wheat flour

2 teaspoons (¼ ounce/7 g) instant yeast

¾ teaspoon salt

1 tablespoon honey

1 tablespoon lightly salted butter, melted

1 large egg, at room temperature, lightly beaten

Poppy seeds, to finish

In a small saucepan, warm the milk and 1 cup (160 ml) of water until lukewarm.

In the bowl of a stand mixer fitted with the dough hook attachment, combine the strong white bread flour, whole wheat flour, yeast, and salt. Pour in the milk mixture, along with the honey and melted butter, and knead on medium-low for about 15 minutes, or until the dough is soft and elastic. Transfer the dough to a lightly oiled bowl, cover with a tea towel, and let rise in a warm spot for about 1 hour, or until doubled in size.

Once the dough has doubled in size, preheat the oven to 400°F (200°C). Line a baking sheet with parchment paper.

Divide the dough into 10 equal pieces and shape into balls. Place the balls of dough on the prepared baking sheet and let rise in a warm spot for 30 minutes.

Brush the tops of the rolls with the lightly beaten egg and sprinkle with the poppy seeds. Bake for about 25 minutes, or until golden brown. Place the rolls on a wire rack to cool. These are best eaten on the day they are baked but will last for up to 2 days in an airtight bag at room temperature.

Hearty Whole Grain Bread

There's nothing quite like the smell of homemade bread. The warmth of the oven envelops the kitchen and you're filled with the anticipation of taking the first bite. Bread is an absolute staple in Norwegian cuisine, with the beloved *skive* — "slice of bread" — acting as a springboard for the many possibilities of an open-faced sandwich. You'll find in Norway, more often than not, an emphasis on hearty breads that rely on a variety of flours, whole grains, and seeds. This loaf incorporates whole flours, where the whole kernel — the bran, germ, and endosperm — are ground into a fine flour, creating a coarser and more nutritious product. The seeds on top offer a nice bit of texture, and you can mix and match to your preference or leave them out altogether. If you like a little sweetness in your bread, add two tablespoons of honey when you add the water.

Makes 1 loaf

2 cups (240 g) whole wheat flour

2 cups (240 g) strong white bread flour

⅓ cup (40 g) whole rye flour

1 cup (50 g) wheat bran

1 teaspoon (⅛ ounce / 3.5 g) instant yeast

1 teaspoon salt

2 cups (480 ml) warm water

3 tablespoons mixed seeds, such as sunflower, pumpkin, flax, and sesame

In a stand mixer fitted with the dough hook attachment, combine the whole wheat flour, strong white bread flour, whole rye flour, wheat bran, yeast, and salt. Add the warm water and knead on medium-low for about 10 minutes, or until the dough is smooth. Transfer the dough to a lightly oiled bowl, cover with a tea towel, and let rise in a warm spot for about 3 hours.

After about 3 hours, on a lightly floured surface, gently form the dough into a round shape and let rest for 10 minutes.

Butter a 9 x 5 inch (23 x 13 cm) loaf pan. Form the rested dough into an oblong shape and place in the prepared loaf pan. Cover with a tea towel and let rise in a warm spot for about 45 minutes, or until doubled in size.

After about 45 minutes, or once the dough has doubled in size, preheat the oven to 400°F (200°C). Using a pastry brush, brush the top of the dough with water and sprinkle the seeds on top, pressing them gently into the dough to stick. Bake for about 40 minutes, or until golden brown on top. Cool in the tin for 10 minutes, then transfer to a wire rack and let cool completely. Store in an airtight bag at room temperature for up to 2 days.

Farmhouse Oat Bread

Baking at home is something we do for ourselves and it's invigorating. We can experiment with the ingredients we have on hand and make a loaf that fits our mood. One loaf we always return to is this farmhouse oat bread. It's soft, springy, hearty, and has a good crust. It's also the kind of bread that's versatile and works well with everything. I usually eat the first warm slice on its own, just to savor it, and I recommend you do the same.

Makes 2 loaves

1½ cups (150 g) quick-cooking oats, plus more for sprinkling

3⅓ cups (800 ml) lukewarm water

6¾ cups (810 g) strong white bread flour, plus more for dusting

4 teaspoons (½ ounce / 14 g) instant yeast

2 teaspoons salt

2 tablespoons honey

In a large bowl, combine the oats and 1⅓ cups (320 ml) of the lukewarm water and let stand for 30 minutes.

In the bowl of a stand mixer fitted with the dough hook attachment, combine the flour, yeast, and salt. Add the honey, along with the remaining 2 cups (480 ml) of lukewarm water and the soaked oat mixture and knead on low for about 15 minutes, or until the dough is workable and somewhat sticky. Transfer the dough to a lightly buttered bowl, cover with plastic wrap, and refrigerate overnight.

The next day, in the bowl of a stand mixer fitted with the dough hook attachment, knead the dough on medium-low for about 10 minutes, or until smooth.

On a lightly floured surface, divide the dough into 2 equal pieces. Knead the dough lightly with your hands and shape into balls. Dust a baking sheet with flour and place the loaves on top. Dust the tops of the loaves with flour. Cover with a damp tea towel and let rise in a warm spot for about 2 hours, or until doubled in size.

Once the dough has doubled in size, preheat the oven to 475°F (240°C). Bring a kettle or saucepan of water to a boil. Pour the boiling water into a roasting pan until it comes about 1½ inches (4 cm) up the sides and carefully place the pan on the bottom of the oven to create steam for a nice crust.

Use a sharp knife to make decorative cuts on the tops of each loaf. Lightly dust the loaves with flour and sprinkle with a few oats. When the oven is ready, place the loaves on the middle shelf of the oven and bake for about 30 minutes, or until golden brown, being careful when opening the oven door because of the steam. Transfer to a wire rack to cool completely. Store in an airtight bag at room temperature for up to 2 days. Alternatively, place the cooled loaves in airtight bags and freeze for up to 2 months.

Barley and Sea Salt Bread

Sitting by the sea, with long grasses swaying nearby, you can feel and taste the humid breeze seasoning the air with salt. This bread reminds me of that sensation. With the ripples of the waves in each loaf and a sharp bite of sea salt contrasting the earthy barley, it's reminiscent of focaccia and hearty enough to hold up to anything you want to put on top. These rustic loaves are ideal to serve with a variety of dishes, but a bowl of warm fish soup will draw you straight to the waters. If you have access to Norwegian sea salt, I highly recommend using it for this recipe.

Makes 2 loaves

1 cup (120 g) barley flour

4 cups (480 g) strong white bread flour

2 teaspoons (¼ ounce/7 g) instant yeast

1 tablespoon salt

2 tablespoons mild-flavored oil

2 tablespoons lightly salted butter, melted

Sea salt, for finishing

In a large bowl, whisk together the barley flour, strong white bread flour, yeast, and salt. Add 2 cups (480 ml) of water and mix to form a wet dough.

Coat a separate large bowl with the oil—there will be some oil remaining at the bottom of the bowl. Place the dough in the bowl, turning to coat, then cover with a tea towel and let rise in a warm spot for about 2 hours, or until doubled in size.

Once the dough has doubled in size, butter two 9 inch (23 cm) round cake pans.

Fold the dough over from the sides into the middle then divide into 2 equal pieces. Shape each piece into a round and place in the cake pans. Cover with a tea towel and let rise in a warm spot for about 1 hour, or until doubled in size.

Once the dough has doubled in size, preheat the oven to 425°F (220°C).

Lightly oil your hands and use your fingers to make dimples in the tops of the dough, creating deep depressions. Pour the melted butter over the 2 loaves, sprinkle with the sea salt, and bake for about 25 minutes, or until golden brown. Transfer to a wire rack to cool. Store in an airtight bag at room temperature for up to 2 days.

Samisk Thin Bread

The 6th of February is *samenes nasjonaldag*, the national day for the Sami, the northernmost indigenous people of Norway, Sweden, Finland, and the Kola Peninsula of Russia. Their diet of reindeer, fish, and berries, among other things, is characteristic of a lifestyle lived close to nature. One of their traditional breads is *gahkku*, which is cooked on a hot stone or griddle over the fire, giving it a lovely toasted look and flavor. For their national day, we often make their national dish, *bidos*, which is a reindeer stew, and gahkku to serve alongside. I included a variation of this bread in my first cookbook and wanted to also share this *tynnbrød*, or "thin bread," style here. It's soft and subtly sweet thanks to the syrup. Enjoy this with rich soups and stews, as a wrap, and even as is with some butter and a drizzle of honey on top. If cooking this outdoors, keep an eye on the heat, so the bread cooks through with a nice golden color.

Makes 12 thin breads

2 tablespoons lightly salted butter

2 tablespoons Norwegian light syrup or golden syrup

4 cups plus 2 tablespoons (500 g) all-purpose flour

1 teaspoon (⅛ ounce / 3.5 g) instant yeast

1 teaspoon salt

1¼ cups (300 ml) warm water

In a small saucepan, warm the butter and syrup over low heat until the butter is melted.

In the bowl of a stand mixer fitted with the dough hook attachment, combine the flour, yeast, and salt. Add the butter mixture and the warm water and knead on medium for about 5 minutes, or until smooth. Transfer the dough to an oiled bowl, cover with a tea towel, and let rise in a warm spot for 30 to 40 minutes, or until doubled in size.

Once the dough has doubled in size, transfer to a lightly floured surface and divide into 12 equal pieces. Using a rolling pin and more flour as needed to prevent sticking, roll out the dough into circles, each roughly 8 inches (20 cm) in diameter.

Heat a large frying pan or skillet over medium-high heat. Place 1 circle of dough on the dry pan and cook for about 1 minute, or until golden spots start forming on the bottom. Flip the bread over and cook for about 1 minute more, or until golden brown on the other side. Place on a plate and cover with a tea towel to keep warm. Continue cooking the rest of the breads, dusting off any excess flour left in the pan before adding more bread. Serve warm. These are best eaten within a day, but leftovers can be stored in an airtight bag at room temperature for up to 3 days.

Rye Rusks

Kavringer are traditional Norwegian rusks, or dried breads, served with toppings, such as butter, cheese, and jam. You might even find them tossed in a bowl with milk and sugar on top. They're made from *boller*—"buns"—that are slowly dried out in a low oven. These rusks are a little heartier thanks to the rye flour, but you could easily use any of the boller doughs in this cookbook to make a sweeter variation. While easy to put together, they do take some time to finish, so a slow day is perfect for making these. They're delightful next to a cup of coffee or tea, and great to bring along in your backpack for an outdoor snack.

Makes 32 rusks

1¾ cups (210 g) light rye flour

3¼ cups (390 g) all-purpose flour

1 tablespoon granulated sugar

2 teaspoons (¼ ounce / 7 g) instant yeast

1 teaspoon salt

2 tablespoons mild-flavored oil

In a large bowl, whisk together the rye flour, all-purpose flour, sugar, yeast, and salt. Make a well in the center of the dry ingredients, then pour in 2 ¼ cups (540 ml) of water and the oil and stir with a wooden spoon to form a wet dough. Cover with a tea towel and let rise in a warm spot for about 30 minutes, or until doubled in size.

Once the dough has doubled in size, preheat the oven to 425°F (220°C). Line 2 baking sheets with parchment paper.

Using wet hands, scoop out about 16 large pieces of dough then form them into oval or round shapes and place on the prepared baking sheets. Cover with a tea towel and let rise in a warm spot for about 30 minutes, or until doubled in size.

Once the dough has doubled in size, bake for about 10 minutes, or until golden brown. Remove the buns from the oven and let cool slightly on the baking sheet. Lower the oven temperature to 260°F (125°C).

Once they are cool enough to handle, cut the buns lengthwise in half and place, cut side up, back on the prepared baking sheets. Bake, opening the oven door a couple of times to release steam, for 2 to 3 ½ hours, or until the buns are golden and dry. They will become drier after they've cooled. Store in an airtight container at room temperature for a couple of months.

Rustic Spelt Crackers

Crackers are wonderful to have around for when you find yourself needing a snack or an extra nibble on the table to use as a base for your offerings. The best crackers, in my opinion, are homemade and you can flavor them however you like using fresh or dried herbs, edible flowers, spices, and anything else you might fancy. There's also no need to worry about keeping them uniform in shape, because these are meant to be rustic, a loving gesture made by hand. The whole process takes no time at all and soon you'll have a basket of crackers that look like you scoured the countryside gathering the ingredients to make them.

Serves 4 to 6

1½ cups (180 g) white spelt flour

¾ tablespoon dried herbs, such as thyme, sage, and rosemary

1 teaspoon baking powder

¾ teaspoon salt

¼ teaspoon black pepper

3 tablespoons mild-flavored oil, plus more for brushing

Preheat the oven to 450°F (230°C).

In a large bowl, whisk together the flour, dried herbs, baking powder, salt, and pepper. Make a well in the center of the dry ingredients, then pour in ½ cup (120 ml) of water and the oil, and stir with a wooden spoon until combined.

Transfer the dough to a lightly floured surface and knead a few times. Divide the dough into 4 equal pieces. Using a rolling pin and more flour as needed to prevent sticking, roll out each piece into a long and thin oval shape. Place the dough ovals on a baking sheet, fitting as many as you can, and lightly brush the tops with oil. Bake for 6 to 8 minutes, or until golden brown and crispy. Repeat with the remaining dough ovals. Transfer to a wire rack and let cool completely, then break into large pieces. Store in an airtight container at room temperature for up to 2 weeks.

Flatbread

Making *flatbrød* is a labor of love. It takes time, so it's a great excuse to gather a few people together in the kitchen and make a day of it. I've made this recipe more accessible, as it only makes ten flatbreads, but you can easily double or triple the recipe to make more. Use these as you would use crackers, as a base for appetizers, or served next to a dip. They're also fantastic with a spread of butter on top and dipped into a brothy soup. If you use a Norwegian griddle called a *takke*, you can make large flatbreads, but if you use a large frying pan instead, you'll have to make smaller ones.

Makes 10 flatbreads

2 cups plus 1 tablespoon plus 1 teaspoon (250 g) barley flour

2 cups plus 1 tablespoon plus 1 teaspoon (250 g) whole wheat flour

1 cup plus 2 teaspoons (125 g) light rye flour

1 cup plus 2 teaspoons (125 g) all-purpose flour

¾ teaspoon salt

2¼ cups (540 ml) lukewarm water, plus more as needed

In a large bowl, whisk together the barley flour, whole wheat flour, rye flour, all-purpose flour, and salt. Make a well in the center of the dry ingredients, then pour in the lukewarm water, adding a little more as needed, and stir with a wooden spoon to form a soft and pliable dough.

Transfer the dough to a well-floured surface and divide into 10 equal balls, about 4 ounces (112 g) each. If using a large frying pan instead of a takke, divide the dough into 20 balls, about 2 ounces (56 g) each. Using a rolling pin and more all-purpose flour as needed to prevent sticking, roll out each ball of dough into a large, thin, even circle, about 14 inches (36 cm) in diameter or half that size if using a large frying pan. Using a soft-bristled brush, dust any excess flour from both sides of the dough

Heat a takke or large frying pan over medium heat. Put the fan on and open a window if possible. Add 1 circle of dough and cook, flipping a few times, for about 10 minutes, or until golden and stiff—the flatbreads will firm up slightly as they cool. Repeat with the remaining rounds of dough. Serve immediately or let the flatbreads cool then stack and store in a cool, dry place for up to a year.

Carnival Buns

Fastelavn is a carnival tradition that takes place on the cusp of Lent, right before Ash Wednesday. The star of this three-day celebration is a simple freshly baked bun with sweetened cream nestled inside and a generous dousing of confectioners' sugar on top—just enough sugar to crown the lips of the one lucky enough to take a bite. *Fastelavnsboller* are decadent yet simple and they are always served on the Sunday. Sometimes a spread of jam or custard will grace the interior as well, but traditionally the cream should suffice. In Bergen, you'll find the leftover buns warmed up the following day then drenched in cream and sugar, which you are more than welcome to do here—if there are any buns left.

Makes 12 buns

1¼ cups (300 ml) lukewarm milk

2 large eggs, at room temperature

4 cups plus 2 tablespoons (500 g) all-purpose flour, sifted

6 tablespoons (75 g) granulated sugar

2 teaspoons (¼ ounce / 7 g) instant yeast

1 teaspoon ground cardamom

¼ teaspoon salt

½ cup (112 g) lightly salted butter, cut into small pieces

1 cup (240 ml) heavy cream

1¼ tablespoons confectioners' sugar, plus more for serving

In a small bowl, whisk together the lukewarm milk and 1 of the eggs.

In a stand mixer fitted with the dough hook attachment, combine the flour, granulated sugar, yeast, cardamom, and salt. Add the milk mixture and knead on low for 8 minutes. Add the butter and knead on medium for about 5 minutes, or until the dough is very elastic and somewhat moist. Transfer the dough to a lightly buttered bowl, cover with a tea towel, and let rise in a warm spot for about 1 hour, or until doubled in size.

Once the dough has doubled in size, preheat the oven to 400°F (200°C). Line a baking sheet with parchment paper.

Divide the dough into 12 equal pieces and use your hands to shape into balls. Place on the prepared baking sheet and let rise in a warm spot for 30 minutes.

In a small bowl, whisk the remaining egg. Using a pastry brush, lightly brush the egg on top of the balls of dough. Bake for about 10 minutes, or until golden brown. Transfer to a wire rack to cool completely.

In a large bowl, whip the heavy cream and confectioners' sugar until stiff peaks form.

To serve, cut the buns horizontally in half, then cover the bottoms with some of the whipped cream. Replace the tops and dust generously with confectioners' sugar. Store unfilled buns in an airtight bag at room temperature for up to 2 days.

Thin Pancakes with Bacon and Blueberry Compote

Fleskepannekaker takes the humble Norwegian pancake to the next level. Pieces of fatty *fleske*, "pork," are cooked into the eggy batter as it turns golden. They can be served simply with a couple snips of fresh chives or, my personal favorite, topped with sweet syrup and fruit compote to unite sweet and salty flavors in every mouthful. While you can serve fleskepannekaker anytime of year, it's an ideal dish to serve on *Feitetirsdag*, or "Fat Tuesday," when people all over the globe are feasting on their variation of pancakes.

Makes 6 large pancakes

❖ **FOR THE PANCAKES**

½ pound (about 225 g) bacon, cut into small pieces

1½ cups (180 g) all-purpose flour

½ teaspoon salt

2 cups plus 1 tablespoon plus 1 teaspoon (500 ml) milk

4 large eggs, at room temperature

Lightly salted butter, for frying

❖ **FOR THE BLUEBERRY COMPOTE**

2 cups (200 g) frozen blueberries

1 tablespoon Norwegian light syrup or golden syrup, plus more for serving

For the pancakes, in a large nonstick frying pan, cook the bacon pieces over medium heat until brown and crispy or to your desired texture. Set aside.

In a large bowl, whisk together the flour and salt. Slowly pour in the milk, a little at a time, until the batter is smooth without any lumps. Whisk in the eggs until fully combined. Let the batter swell for 15 to 20 minutes.

For the blueberry compote, in a small saucepan, bring the blueberries and syrup to a gentle simmer over medium heat. Continue simmering for about 10 minutes, or until thickened. Set aside.

Heat a large frying pan or skillet over medium heat, then add some butter and let it melt and coat the bottom of the pan. Ladle in some of the batter, moving the pan around to evenly coat the bottom. Top with a good handful of the cooked bacon pieces. You should get about 6 pancakes, so divide the bacon pieces accordingly. Cook until the bottom of the pancake has set and turned golden in color. Turn over with a spatula, being careful, as some of the bacon pieces might be loose, and finish cooking the other side. Fold the pancake in half, and then in half again, making a nice triangle. Transfer the pancake to a plate, toss any loose bacon pieces on top, and cover with foil to keep warm. Continue this process until all the batter has been used up.

Serve warm with a good dollop of the blueberry compote and a drizzle of syrup on top. Store leftovers covered in the refrigerator for up to 3 days.

Tropical Aroma Cake

With its mix of warm spices, coffee, and chocolate, this incredibly moist marble cake will have you drifting off into your own personal paradise. It's a classic cake, first appearing around the 1920s, and one reserved for special occasions. I often make it in February for Mother's Day in Norway. You can bake a small four-layer cake or a larger two-layer cake—either will be dreamy.

Serves 8 to 10

❖ **FOR THE CAKE**

2¼ cups (270 g) all-purpose flour

2 teaspoons baking powder

1 teaspoon ground cinnamon

1 teaspoon ground nutmeg, plus fresh nutmeg shavings for finishing

1 tablespoon cocoa powder, plus more for finishing

1 tablespoon hot water

1¼ cups plus 2 tablespoons (220 g) dark brown sugar

½ cup (112 g) lightly salted butter, at room temperature

2 large eggs, at room temperature

1 cup (240 ml) milk

❖ **FOR THE GLAZE**

2 cups (240 g) confectioners' sugar

5 tablespoons (75 ml) strong hot coffee

2 tablespoons lightly salted butter, at room temperature

1½ tablespoons cocoa powder

½ teaspoon vanilla extract

For the cake, preheat the oven to 350°F (180°C). Butter four 6 inch (15 cm) springform pans or two 9 inch (23 cm) springform pans.

In a medium bowl, whisk together the flour, baking powder, cinnamon, and nutmeg.

In a small bowl, whisk together the cocoa powder and hot water.

In the bowl of a stand mixer fitted with the paddle attachment, beat the brown sugar and butter until light and fluffy. Add the eggs and beat for 2 to 3 minutes, or until light and creamy. Add the flour mixture and blend. Add the milk and beat until just blended. Transfer a third of the batter to a medium bowl and stir in the cocoa mixture—you should now have one-third chocolate batter and two-thirds plain batter.

Divide the plain batter between the 4 smaller prepared pans or the 2 larger prepared pans. Divide the chocolate batter between the pans, pouring it on top of the plain batter. Using a toothpick, swirl the chocolate batter into the plain batter, creating a marble effect. Bake for 15 to 20 minutes if using 4 smaller pans and 20 to 25 minutes if using 2 larger pans, or until the tops are golden brown and a toothpick inserted in the center comes out clean. Cool slightly in the pans before transferring to a wire rack to cool completely.

For the glaze, whisk together the confectioners' sugar, hot coffee, butter, cocoa powder, and vanilla until smooth.

To assemble a small 4-layer cake, place 1 cake layer on a serving plate. Pour a quarter of the glaze on top, spreading it to the edges of the cake. Arrange the second cake layer on top and repeat the process of adding the glaze. Arrange the third cake layer on top and repeat again. Top with the final cake layer and spread the remaining glaze on the top and sides of the cake. To assemble a large 2-layer cake, place 1 cake layer, bottom side facing upwards, on a serving plate. Pour half of the glaze on top, spreading it to the edges of the cake. Top with the other cake layer, bottom side down, and spread the remaining glaze on the top and sides of the cake. Dust the top with cocoa powder and fresh nutmeg shavings before serving. Keep covered in the refrigerator for up to 3 days.

Cinnamon Cake Bread

I remember the first time I bit into this delicate and soft yet subtly dense cake adorned with a layer of cinnamon sugar. It was an informal setting—an auditorium filled with proud parents and excitable children celebrating a season of skiing. Irresistible cakes and cookies were sprawled out on tables, but I was drawn to the understated cake with a cinnamon sugar crown. It was simple in every way yet anything but simple when it came to taste. It remained with me, this *kanelkake*, or "cinnamon cake."

I'm not sure of the origins of kanelkake or when it became one of the many cakes served throughout Norway. I do know it's a familiar favorite and an ideal cake to share with others. Rather than bake it as a traditional round cake, I veered toward my loaf pans and tweaked it to have a lovely swirl of cinnamon sugar throughout the center and on top, which hardens as it cooks providing a delectable, cracked crust. This recipe easily doubles, so you could always keep one and give the other away as a tasty gift.

Makes 1 loaf (about 10 slices)

❖ **FOR THE CAKE**

2¼ cups (270 g) all-purpose flour

1 cup (200 g) granulated sugar

2 teaspoons baking powder

½ teaspoon salt

2 large eggs, at room temperature

1 cup (240 ml) buttermilk

¼ cup (60 ml) mild-flavored oil

❖ **FOR THE FILLING AND TOPPING**

6 tablespoons (75 g) granulated sugar

¾ tablespoon ground cinnamon

For the cake, preheat the oven to 350°F (180°C). Butter a 9 x 5 inch (23 x 13 cm) loaf pan.

In a large bowl, whisk together the flour, sugar, baking powder, and salt.

In a medium bowl, whisk together the eggs, buttermilk, and oil. Pour this into the flour mixture and blend well.

For the filling and topping, in a small bowl, whisk together the sugar and cinnamon.

Pour half of the batter into the prepared loaf pan. Sprinkle half of the cinnamon sugar evenly on top of the batter. Pour the remaining batter on top of the cinnamon sugar, then sprinkle with the remaining cinnamon sugar. Bake for 50 to 60 minutes, or until a toothpick inserted in the center comes out clean. Let the cake cool in the pan for 10 minutes, transfer to a wire rack, and let cool completely. Store in an airtight container at room temperature for up to 3 days.

Juniper Berry Sugar "Cabin" Buns

The lingering winter invites many trips to the *hytte*—"cabin." I was inspired to make these buns for a way to indulge, while still having time to fit in activities outside of the kitchen. With their lavishly buttery layers and syrupy bottoms, they're similar to morning buns but are made using a simpler process. The dough is prepped the night before and assembled in the morning. While the buns are rising, you can head to the slopes or take a nice lingering walk. Juniper, with its piney flavors, is a subtle nod to the mountains and the feeling of escape.

Makes 12 buns

❖ FOR THE BUNS

¾ cup plus 1 tablespoon
   (200 ml) milk

5 cups (600 g) all-purpose flour

6 tablespoons (65 g) dark brown
   sugar

2 teaspoons (¼ ounce / 7 g)
   instant yeast

½ teaspoon salt

1 cup (224 g) lightly salted butter,
   chilled

❖ FOR THE JUNIPER SUGAR

1½ tablespoons juniper berries,
   finely crushed

1½ cups (300 g) superfine sugar

For the buns, in a small saucepan, heat the milk and 1¼ cups (300 ml) of water until lukewarm. Pour the mixture into the bowl of a stand mixer fitted with the dough hook attachment. Add the flour, brown sugar, yeast, and salt. Mix on low until combined, then knead on medium for about 10 minutes, or until elastic and somewhat moist. Transfer the dough to a well-floured surface. Using a rolling pin and more flour as needed to prevent sticking, roll out the dough into a long rectangle that measures roughly 32 x 10 inches (80 x 25 cm) with the long sides horizontal.

Using a cheese slicer or mandoline slicer, thinly slice the butter. Place the slices evenly over the dough. Working from left to right, fold the dough equally 6 times until you have a rectangle that has 7 layers and is about 5 inches (12.5 cm) wide. Turn the dough 90 degrees and roll into a long rectangle that measures roughly 32 x 10 inches (80 x 25 cm) with the long sides horizontal. Fold the dough again, from left to right, 6 times. Place in a wide container, loosely cover, and refrigerate overnight.

For the juniper sugar, in a medium bowl, combine the crushed juniper berries and superfine sugar. Cover and set aside until ready to use.

The next day, place the dough on a floured surface. Using a rolling pin and more flour as needed to prevent sticking, roll out the dough into a large rectangle that measures roughly 18 x 10 inches (45 x 25 cm). Sprinkle 1 cup (200 g) of the juniper sugar on top. Starting with 1 of the long sides, roll the dough around the filling to form a long, roughly 18 inch (45 cm), log. Using a sharp knife, cut the dough crosswise into 12 equal pieces.

Butter a muffin pan and sprinkle some of the remaining juniper sugar inside, shaking off the excess. Carefully place the buns, cut side up, in the prepared muffin pan then cover with a tea towel and let rise in a warm spot for 1½ hours.

Preheat the oven to 375°F (190°C).

Bake the buns for about 25 minutes, or until golden brown on top. Let cool in the pan for 5 minutes. Remove the buns from the pan and dip the tops in the remaining juniper sugar. Set on a wire rack to cool slightly before serving. These are best eaten on the day they are baked, but leftovers can be stored in an airtight container at room temperature for up to 2 days.

Pull-Apart Bun Bread with Whipped Honey Butter

I adore the concept of pull-apart bread. It's inviting and interactive, a centerpiece that encourages conversation as each buttery piece of yeasty bread tears from the other. I've used traditional *bolle* — "bun" — dough and added whipped honey butter that soaks into the bread as it puffs up and bakes in the hot oven. You can be even bolder and add in some fruit pieces if you feel so inclined.

Serves 6 to 10

❖ FOR THE BUN BREAD

4 cups (480 g) all-purpose flour

¼ cup (50 g) granulated sugar

2 teaspoons (¼ ounce / 7 g) instant yeast

1 teaspoon ground cardamom

¼ teaspoon salt

¾ cup (180 ml) lukewarm milk

⅓ cup (75 g) lightly salted butter, melted

2 large eggs, at room temperature

❖ FOR THE WHIPPED HONEY BUTTER

1 cup (224 g) lightly salted butter, at room temperature

½ cup (120 ml) runny honey

For the bun bread, in the bowl of a stand mixer fitted with the dough hook attachment, combine the flour, sugar, yeast, cardamom, and salt. Add the lukewarm milk, melted butter, and the eggs and knead on low for 8 to 10 minutes, or until the dough is very elastic and somewhat moist. Transfer the dough to a lightly buttered bowl, cover with a tea towel, and let rise in a warm spot for about 40 minutes, or until doubled in size.

For the whipped honey butter, in a medium bowl, combine the butter and honey and blend until smooth.

Once the dough has doubled in size, preheat the oven to 350°F (180°C). Butter a 9 x 5 inch (23 x 13 cm) loaf pan.

On a lightly floured surface, using a rolling pin and more flour as needed to prevent sticking, roll out the dough into a large rectangle that measures roughly 20 x 12 inches (50 x 30 cm). Spread half of the honey butter over the entire surface of the dough, spreading it to the edges. Cut the dough into 20 equal squares. Stack a couple of squares together and place them upright in the prepared loaf tin. Continue until all the squares are placed inside and tightly packed—there will be some space left in the pan, which will fill in when the dough rises. Cover the dough with a tea towel and let rise in a warm spot for about 30 minutes, or until doubled in size.

Once the dough has doubled in size, bake for 35 to 40 minutes, or until golden brown. Brush some of the honey butter on top then let cool in the pan for 20 minutes. Serve warm with the remaining honey butter. Store leftovers in an airtight container at room temperature for up to 2 days.

New Light

❖   Nytt lys

❖ **THERE'S A CHANGE IN THE AIR.** It's subtle yet very much there. The light seems brighter, as the earth breathes in a new way, each inhale inviting a promise of the life to come. Optimism coats the air, enveloping everything in its path. The spring equinox marks a transition, from the cold and frigid winter to warmer days and fresh growth.

Winters in Norway are long, and spring shares its bed with both snowfall and fresh buds. *Påske* (Easter) falls on or right after the spring equinox, marking the start of the season when a trip to the cabin to spend a week skiing is just as important as the tulips adorning the table. Easter cakes and breads feature golden custards and creams and are often brightened with citrus or enriched with chocolate.

Following Påske, May arrives as the unofficial "cake month," with Norway's Constitution Day at its heart, along with confirmations, baptisms, and weddings. Tables lined with inviting treats from almond cookie towers to meringue covered sponge cakes are no longer confined indoors, as the landscape that was recently white and barren is finally green and flourishing. Winter is now a fleeting thought and this is the start of the growing season, a jubilant time when nature gifts us with a mosaic of delectable goods you need to grab while you can before they fade away yet again.

Success Tart

Suksessterte has won the hearts of many with its rich flavor, irresistible macaron bottom, and bright yellow hue. The fact that it's gluten free and features a simple custard whipped with a generous amount of butter doesn't hurt either. While served for celebrations year-round, suksessterte has a special place at *Påske* (Easter). Its golden color and use of eggs make it particularly suitable for this time of year. Even nature tends to nod in agreement with the first bulbs of spring sprouting yellow.

Serves 8 to 10

1¾ cups (210 g) almonds

5 large eggs, at room temperature, separated

1⅔ cups (200 g) confectioners' sugar

¾ cup plus 1 tablespoon (200 ml) heavy cream

¾ cup (150 g) granulated sugar

1 teaspoon vanilla extract

⅔ cup (150 g) lightly salted butter, at room temperature

3½ ounces (100 g) dark chocolate

Preheat the oven to 350°F (180°C). Cut a round piece of parchment paper so it fits perfectly in the bottom of a 9 inch (23 cm) springform pan. Butter the pan, then add the parchment and butter it.

In a food processor, pulse the almonds until coarsely ground.

In a stand mixer fitted with the whisk attachment, whip the egg whites on medium until stiff peaks form. Sift the confectioners' sugar over the egg whites, then add the ground almonds, and use a spatula to gently fold until just combined. Pour the batter into the prepared pan and bake for 25 to 30 minutes, or until golden brown. Let cool completely in the pan, then transfer to a serving plate.

In a medium saucepan, combine the egg yolks, heavy cream, granulated sugar, and vanilla over medium heat and bring to a boil, stirring constantly. Lower the heat and simmer for about 5 minutes, or until thickened. Let cool completely.

In a stand mixer fitted with the whisk attachment, whip the butter on low until smooth. Add the cooled cream mixture and whip for about 1 minute, or until combined and fluffy. Pour on top of the cooled macaron bottom.

In a small saucepan, bring some water to a boil over medium-high heat. Place a heatproof bowl on top, making sure the bowl doesn't touch the water. Add the chocolate to the bowl and let melt, stirring frequently. Remove from the heat and drizzle the melted chocolate over the top of the cake. Serve right away or refrigerate for 1 hour to set the chocolate. Store covered in the refrigerator for up to 1 week or freeze for up to 3 months.

Whole Wheat, Chocolate, and Orange Braided Bread

I created this sweet bread with *Påske* (Easter) in mind to capture the Norwegian admiration for and tradition of eating chocolate and oranges at this time of year. Taking candied orange peels and dark chocolate, I pair them with a soft and hearty whole wheat dough that has a hint of cardamom. The outcome is sweet but not overly so, with gooey chocolate complimented by bright bursts of orange. Plan on making the candied peels at least a day ahead.

Makes 2 breads; serves 20

❖ FOR THE CANDIED ORANGE
  PEELS

3 large oranges

1½ cups (300 g) granulated sugar

❖ FOR THE DOUGH

2½ cups (600 ml) milk

⅔ cup (150 g) lightly salted butter

2½ cups (300 g) whole wheat flour

5 cups (600 g) all-purpose flour

¾ cup (150 g) granulated sugar

4 teaspoons (½ ounce / 14 g)
  instant yeast

1 teaspoon salt

2 tablespoons freshly grated
  orange zest

1 large egg, at room temperature,
  beaten

❖ FOR THE FILLING

1 cup (200 g) granulated sugar

½ cup (50 g) cocoa powder

2 tablespoons ground cardamom

¾ cup plus 2 tablespoons
  (200 g) lightly salted butter, at
  room temperature

7 ounces (200 g) dark chocolate,
  finely chopped

For the candied orange peels, cut the ends off the oranges then cut the peel of each orange into 4 vertical sections. Peel away each section from the flesh and cut the sections into long thin strips that are roughly ¼ inch (6 mm) thick. Reserve the orange flesh for another use. Put the strips in a medium heavy-bottomed saucepan, then cover with cold water and bring to a simmer over medium-high heat. Continue simmering for 15 minutes. Drain the peels and rinse thoroughly with cold water.

In the same saucepan, combine the sugar and 1½ cups (360 ml) of water and cook over medium-high heat, stirring occasionally, until the sugar is dissolved. Lower the heat, add the peels, and simmer, uncovered, for about 45 minutes, or until the peels are translucent. Remove the peels with a slotted spoon, transfer to a wire rack, and let dry for 24 to 48 hours. Reserve the syrup for another use. Once the peels are dried, cut them into small pieces.

For the dough, in a small saucepan, warm the milk and butter over low heat until the butter is melted. Pour into a stand mixer fitted with the dough hook attachment. Add the whole wheat flour, all-purpose flour, sugar, yeast, salt, and orange zest and knead on medium-low for about 8 minutes, or until the dough is soft and elastic. Transfer the dough to a lightly buttered bowl, cover with a tea towel, and let rise in a warm spot for about 1 hour, or until doubled in size.

For the filling, in a large bowl, whisk together the sugar, cocoa powder, and cardamom. Add the butter and combine to form a smooth paste.

Once the dough has doubled in size, on a lightly floured surface, divide the dough into 2 equal pieces. Using a rolling pin and more flour as needed to prevent sticking, roll out 1 piece of dough into a large rectangle that measures roughly 22 x 18 inches (55 x 45 cm). Using a rubber spatula, spread half of the filling across the dough, going all the way to the edges. Sprinkle half of the chopped chocolate on top, followed by half of the candied orange peel pieces. Starting with 1 of the long sides, roll the dough around the filling to form a long, roughly 22 inch (55 cm), log.   →

Using a sharp knife, cut the log lengthwise in half. Place the 2 halves next to each other, cut side facing up, and braid them by alternating each dough half over the other, keeping the open layers on top. Pinch the ends together to seal. Take one end of the braid and roll it tightly inwards to create a snail shape. Tuck the other end under the dough and pinch to seal. Repeat this process with the other piece of dough and the rest of the filling, chopped chocolate, and candied orange peel pieces. Line 2 baking sheets with parchment paper and place the breads on top. Cover with a tea towel and let rise in a warm spot for 40 minutes.

After 40 minutes, preheat the oven to 375°F (190°C).

Brush the tops of the dough with the beaten egg and press any candied orange peel pieces that are sticking out into the dough to prevent burning. Bake for 27 to 30 minutes, or until golden brown on top. Let cool slightly before serving. Store in an airtight container at room temperature for up to 2 days or in the freezer for up to 2 months.

Danish Pastries with Orange and Vanilla Custard

The smell of melting butter amidst flaky dough with a slight hint of orange and vanilla reminds me of spring, because it's during *Påske* (Easter), when oranges are ever present, that I make these gorgeous pastries. Layering the dough may seem like busy work, but the process is quite easy to do. You'll end up with leftover custard to serve alongside the pastries or you can just grab a spoon and dig in while these are baking.

Makes 20 pastries

❖ **FOR THE DOUGH**

4 cups plus 2 tablespoons (500 g) all-purpose flour

3 tablespoons granulated sugar

4 teaspoons (½ ounce / 14 g) instant yeast

1¼ cups (300 ml) whole milk

1 large egg, at room temperature

1 cup (224 g) lightly salted butter, cold

❖ **FOR THE CUSTARD**

½ cup (100 g) granulated sugar

4 large egg yolks, at room temperature

3 tablespoons cornstarch

2 cups (480 ml) whole milk

1 teaspoon orange zest

2 tablespoons freshly squeezed orange juice

½ vanilla bean, split lengthwise, or 1 teaspoon vanilla extract

For the dough, in the bowl of a stand mixer fitted with the paddle attachment, combine the flour, sugar, yeast, milk, and egg and knead on medium for about 5 minutes, or until soft and smooth. Cover with a tea towel and let stand for 10 minutes.

For the custard, in a large bowl, whisk together the sugar and egg yolks. Add the cornstarch and whisk until thick and pale yellow.

In a small saucepan, combine the milk with the orange zest and juice. Scrape the seeds from the vanilla bean into the milk and add the scraped bean (or add the vanilla extract). Warm over medium heat until just beginning to simmer then remove from the heat. Remove the vanilla bean, then slowly add the milk to the egg yolk mixture, whisking constantly to avoid curdling the eggs. Pour the mixture back into the saucepan and place over medium heat. Cook, stirring constantly, until thick. Set aside to cool.

Preheat the oven to 425°F (220°C). Line 2 baking sheets with parchment paper.

Transfer the dough to a lightly floured surface. Using a rolling pin and more flour as needed to prevent sticking, roll out the dough into a large rectangle that measures roughly 24 x 16 inches (60 x 40 cm) with the long sides horizontal.

Using a cheese slicer or mandoline slicer, thinly slice the butter. Place the slices evenly over the left two-thirds of the dough. Fold the section of dough without butter over the middle third, and fold again over the last third, creating a rectangle with 3 layers of dough and 2 layers of butter. Turn the dough 90 degrees and roll out into a ½ inch (1.25 cm) thick rectangle. Repeat the folding process again to create 3 layers, then turn the dough 90 degrees.   →

Roll out and fold the dough again for a total of 3 times, then roll out the dough into a rectangle that measures roughly 20 x 10 inches (50 x 25 cm) with the long sides horizontal. Cut the dough horizontally into twenty ½ inch (1.25 cm) thick strips. Roll a strip of dough around the tops of your middle 3 fingers, leaving about 4 inches (10 cm) of dough to loop over the top and then tuck under to create a knot shape. Repeat to make more pastries. Place the pastries on the prepared baking sheets and top each pastry with a spoonful of custard. Bake for 12 to 15 minutes, or until golden brown and flaky. Transfer the pastries to a wire rack to cool before serving. These are best on the day they are made but will keep stored in an airtight container at room temperature for up to 2 days.

Bergen Pretzels

Vannkringler are a well-known type of pretzel, which come from Bergen, and are thought to be influenced by Dutch and German salesman who were operating in Bryggen, an old trading wharf in Bergen, during the Hanseatic period. Being easy to store and having a long shelf life, vannkringler were purchased by many fishermen, who would take them along on their journeys, sometimes storing them in empty wooden caskets as they headed back home.

Vannkringler also happen to be a permanent fixture on Norway's Constitution Day, when they find their place on the table alongside *spekemat*, which refers to cured meats, and *rømmegrøt*, or "sour cream porridge." The recipe is simple—just flour, water, yeast, salt, and butter—but the technique is artful, as the dough is rolled out thinly and then tossed and twisted around before being sealed with a gentle press. The pretzels are then placed in a hot water bath and baked until golden brown, making them buttery and soft yet crispy on the outside. They are best fresh but can be stored.

Makes 16 pretzels

3½ cups (420 g) all-purpose flour

2 teaspoons (¼ ounce / 7 g)
  instant yeast

¼ teaspoon salt

1 cup (240 ml) warm water

6 tablespoons (84 g) lightly salted
  butter, melted

Sea salt, for finishing

In a stand mixer fitted with the dough hook attachment, combine the flour, yeast, salt, warm water, and melted butter and knead on medium-low for about 8 minutes, or until the dough is soft and pliable. Transfer the dough to a lightly buttered bowl, cover with a tea towel, and let rise in a warm spot for about 1 hour, or until doubled in size.

Once the dough has doubled in size, preheat the oven to 425°F (220°C). Butter a large baking sheet.

Divide the dough into 16 equal pieces. On a clean surface, roll out each piece of dough into a long and thin rope, about 18 inches (45 cm) long. Form each dough rope into a U-shape, then twist the ends together. Bring the twisted ends back down over the bottom of the U-shape and press down to form a pretzel shape.

Bring a medium saucepan filled with water to a boil over medium-high heat. Working in batches of 2, simmer the pretzels for 1 minute, or until they float to the top. Transfer to the prepared baking sheet and sprinkle the tops of the pretzels with sea salt. Repeat to simmer the rest of the pretzels. Bake for 15 to 18 minutes, or until lightly golden. Transfer to a wire rack to cool. Store in an airtight container at room temperature for up to 1 week.

Soft Spelt Potato Flatbreads

If grilling is on the menu, then *lomper* make an appearance. These soft flatbreads are considered a small variety of potato-based *lefse*, and you'll find *pølse i lompe* — "a hot dog wrapped in a lompe" — a frequent offer around this time of year. In fact, more hot dogs are consumed on May 17th, Norway's Constitution Day, than any other day of the year, which averages to about two and half sausages per person. When served, you can have your hot dog wrapped in a bun or a lompe. They're simple to make at home and are incredibly versatile. I also make lomper in the summer, when the tomatoes are ripe, and serve them with roasted tomatoes and caramelized onions (page 153).

Makes 10 lomper

1½ pounds (650 g) starchy
  potatoes, such as russet,
  Kerr's Pink, or Beate

½ teaspoon salt

1 cup (120 g) white spelt flour

In a large pot, cover the potatoes with cold salted water and bring to a boil. Lower the heat and simmer for about 20 minutes, or until the potatoes are tender when pierced with a knife. Drain the potatoes and cool slightly. Peel the potatoes, combine with the salt, and run through a ricer into a large bowl or mash by hand until completely smooth. Mix in the flour; the dough should be soft.

Divide the dough into 2 ounce (56 g) balls—there should be about 10.

On a floured surface, using a rolling pin and more flour as needed to prevent sticking, gently roll out each ball of dough into an 8 inch (20 cm) round. Use a plate or bowl to help shape the rounds into even circles or leave them as is for a more rustic look. Use a soft-bristled brush to brush off any excess flour then use a fork to poke a couple holes in the dough to prevent it from bubbling up while cooking.

Heat a *takke* to medium-high heat or place a large frying pan directly on the stove over medium-high heat. Put the fan on and open a window if possible. Gently place 1 lompe on the dry, hot takke or pan and cook for about 30 seconds, or until golden brown on the bottom. Flip the lompe and cook for about 30 seconds or until golden brown on the other side. Place the cooked lompe on a plate and cover completely with plastic wrap, followed by a tea towel, to keep the lompe soft and moist. Brush any excess flour from the takke or pan so it doesn't burn. Continue making lomper, using the remaining dough and stacking them on top of each other under the plastic wrap and tea towel. The lomper can be served immediately or wrapped in plastic and refrigerated for up to 5 days.

World's Best Cake

A simple vanilla sponge baked with meringue and almonds becomes the centerpiece of this dreamy layer cake filled with custard and whipped cream. *Kvæfjordkake* has earned its title of *verdens beste*, or "world's best," in the eyes of most Norwegians and those who have had the pleasure of eating it. It's reserved for celebrations, and rightly so. But this is not a difficult cake to make, and you can make it a day in advance to let the flavors come together even more.

Serves 12

❖ **FOR THE CAKE**

1¼ cups (150 g) all-purpose flour

1½ teaspoons baking powder

½ cup (112 g) lightly salted butter, at room temperature

½ cup plus 2 tablespoons (125 g) granulated sugar

4 large egg yolks, at room temperature

¼ cup (60 ml) milk

1 teaspoon vanilla extract

❖ **FOR THE MERINGUE**

4 large egg whites, at room temperature

1 cup (200 g) granulated sugar

½ cup (50 g) sliced almonds

❖ **FOR THE CUSTARD**

¼ cup (50 g) granulated sugar

2 large egg yolks, at room temperature

2 tablespoons cornstarch

2 cups (480 ml) whole milk

½ vanilla bean, split lengthwise, or 1 teaspoon vanilla extract

❖ **FOR THE WHIPPED CREAM**

1¼ cups (300 ml) heavy cream

For the cake, preheat the oven to 325°F (165°C). Butter a 16 x 12 inch (40 x 30 cm) rimmed baking sheet and line it with parchment paper, pressing down so the parchment sticks to the baking sheet.

In a medium bowl, whisk together the flour and baking powder.

In the bowl of a stand mixer fitted with the paddle attachment, beat the butter and sugar together until light and fluffy. Add the egg yolks, 1 at a time, beating until incorporated. Add the milk and vanilla and beat until blended. Add the flour mixture, beating until incorporated; the batter should be somewhat thick and sticky. Using a rubber spatula, carefully spread the batter evenly across the prepared baking sheet, going as far to the edges as possible, while maintaining a rectangular shape.

For the meringue, in a stand mixer fitted with the whisk attachment, whip the egg whites on medium until foamy. Gradually add the sugar, whipping until glossy stiff peaks form. Pour the meringue over the batter on the baking sheet and use a spatula to spread it evenly, lifting upwards to form little peaks. Sprinkle the sliced almonds on top. Bake for about 30 minutes, or until the meringue is dry and lightly golden. Set aside to cool.

For the custard, in a large bowl, whisk together the sugar and egg yolks. Add the cornstarch and whisk until thick and pale yellow.

Put the milk in a small saucepan. Scrape the seeds from the vanilla bean into the milk and add the scraped bean (or add the vanilla extract). Warm over medium heat until just beginning to simmer then remove from the heat. Remove the vanilla bean, then slowly add the milk to the egg yolk mixture, whisking constantly to avoid curdling the eggs. Pour the mixture back into the saucepan and place over medium heat. Cook, stirring constantly, until thick. Set aside to cool.

For the whipped cream, whip the heavy cream until stiff peaks form. Fold into the cooled custard.   →

To assemble, use the parchment paper to lift the cake out of the baking sheet and place, meringue side up, on a large cutting board with the long sides horizontal. Cut the cake vertically in half so that you have 2 equal size cakes. Carefully hold a large serving tray with 1 hand over the top of 1 of the cakes. Place the other hand under the cake, and flip it over onto the serving tray, so the meringue side is facing down on the tray. Peel away the parchment paper. Spread the custard cream over the cake on the serving tray. Peel away the parchment paper from the other cake and gently place it, meringue side up, on top of the custard cream to form 1 cake. Chill in the refrigerator for an hour or so before serving. Keep covered in the refrigerator for 3 to 4 days.

White Lady Marzipan Cake

You have marzipan cakes and then you have *hvit dame*. "White Lady" is a classic Bergen layer cake with a hazelnut macaron bottom enveloped in delicate marzipan. It is said that the name came from a German emperor who visited the city often. He was served this cake at every visit and one day announced, *"Ah, nochmal die weiße Dame,"* which translates to, "Ah, again the white lady"—a famous ghost in Germany. The name remained and today this gorgeous cake is a must at celebrations.

Serves 10 to 12

❖ **FOR THE MACARON BOTTOM**

2 tablespoons plus 2 teaspoons
   all-purpose flour

¾ cup (80 g) ground hazelnuts

¾ cup (150 g) granulated sugar

2 large egg whites, at room
   temperature

❖ **FOR THE CAKE**

6 large eggs, at room temperature

¾ cup plus 2 tablespoons (175 g)
   granulated sugar

1½ cups (180 g) all-purpose flour

1 teaspoon baking powder

3 cups (720 ml) heavy cream

3 tablespoons confectioners' sugar,
   plus more for serving

17½ ounces (500 g) marzipan

¾ cup (200 g) apricot or strawberry
   jam

For the macaron bottom, preheat the oven to 225°F (110°C). Line the bottoms of two 9 inch (23 cm) springform pans with parchment paper then butter the paper and the sides of the pan.

In a large bowl, whisk together the flour, hazelnuts, and ½ cup (100 g) of the granulated sugar.

In a stand mixer fitted with the whisk attachment, whip the egg whites on medium until foamy. Gradually add the remaining ¼ cup (50 g) of granulated sugar, whipping until stiff peaks form. Using a rubber spatula, gently fold the méringue into the flour mixture. Pour into 1 of the prepared pans and bake for 50 to 60 minutes, or until cooked through. Let cool completely in the pan.

For the cake, increase the oven temperature to 350°F (180°C).

In a stand mixer fitted with the whisk attachment, whip the eggs and granulated sugar on medium-high for 6 to 8 minutes, or until stiff and light in color. Sift the flour and baking powder over the batter and use a spatula to gently fold until just combined. Pour into the other prepared pan and set on a baking sheet. Bake for about 35 minutes, or until golden brown. Let cool completely in the pan.

Whip the heavy cream and confectioners' sugar until stiff peaks form.

Lightly dust your work surface and rolling pin with confectioners' sugar. Flatten the marzipan into a round disk and roll out into a large circle that's roughly ⅛ inch (3 mm) thick.

To assemble, loosen the macaron bottom from the springform pan. Gently place a serving platter on top of the macaron bottom and carefully turn it over. Peel away the parchment paper.

Cut the cake horizontally into 2 even layers. Spread a generous amount of jam on 1 layer, then gently turn the cake over and place it on top of the macaron bottom, so the jam side is directly on top of the macaron. Spread a layer of jam on the top of the cake followed by half of the whipped cream, spreading it to the edges of the cake. Place the remaining cake layer on top, followed with a layer of jam. Cover the top and sides with the remaining whipped cream. Carefully drape the marzipan over the top of the cake, gently smoothing the top and sides. Cut away any excess marzipan from the bottom. Refrigerate for a few hours to let the flavors come together. When ready to serve, dust with confectioners' sugar. Keep covered in the refrigerator for up to 3 days.

Almond Wreath Cake

Almond-based rings rise into a tower of confectionary delight with this festive cake. *Kransekake*, or "wreath cake," is served on Norway's Constitution Day, as well as for Christmas, weddings, baptisms, and confirmations. The dough is made from ground almonds, confectioners' sugar, and egg whites, making it naturally gluten free. If you can't find kransekake forms, you can trace your own by hand or forego them altogether and roll out small pieces of dough into finger shapes to make cookies that are baked exactly as described below. The dough needs to chill overnight, so plan to make it the day before. This is also a great cake to freeze as it will last for quite some time.

Makes 18 rings; serves about 40

❖ **FOR THE CAKE**

4¼ cups (510 g) skin-on or blanched almonds, finely ground

4¼ cups (510 g) confectioners' sugar

4 large egg whites, lightly beaten and at room temperature,

Semolina (optional)

❖ **FOR THE GLAZE**

1 large egg white, at room temperature

1⅔ cups (200 g) confectioners' sugar

For the cake, in a large bowl, blend the ground almonds and confectioners' sugar. Add the egg whites and use your hands to combine well. Cover and refrigerate overnight.

The next day, preheat the oven to 400°F (200°C).

Use a pastry brush to generously grease 18 kransekake forms with melted butter or baking spray. Pour semolina over the forms, turning to coat, then shake off any excess over a bowl (omit the semolina altogether to keep the cake gluten free).

On an un-floured surface, take a handful of the dough and work it in your hands. Roll it out into a long, even sausage, about the thickness of a finger. You want the dough to be a little thinner than the form itself, so that when it bakes and expands, it doesn't go over the form. Place the dough into a form, cutting it to fit and blending the ends together with your fingers. Shake and tap the form gently to move the dough a little to help prevent sticking. Repeat with the rest of the dough to make 17 more kransekake rings, rolling out the dough into varying lengths as necessary. Place as many kransekake rings as you can on a baking sheet and bake for about 10 minutes, or until just turning golden. Repeat until all the kransekake rings are baked. Let the kransekake rings cool completely in their forms before gently removing them and brushing off any excess semolina.

For the glaze, in a small bowl, whisk together the egg white and confectioners' sugar to create a somewhat thick glaze. Transfer to a piping bag fitted with a small round pastry tip.

Organize the rings by size. Starting with the largest ring, pipe the glaze on top, going back and forth to make a zigzag design. Stack the second largest ring on top and pipe the glaze on top. Repeat until you've layered all the rings into a tower.

To serve, pull or break off the rings. Store leftovers in an airtight container at room temperature or wrap well and freeze; defrost at room temperature before serving.

Prince Cake

Prince cake features a luscious shortbread pastry with a rich and moist almond filling and is as indulgent as the name suggests. Its origins trace back to Erichsens Konditori, a confectionery in Trondheim, where a Belgium pastry apprentice brought the recipe to Norway around 1860. Although everyone knew what the ingredients were, the mixing ratios were a closely guarded secret that only the pastry chef knew—he weighed the ingredients the night before when the bakers had gone home. While the original recipe is now widely known, there are similar variations all over. This is such an exquisite cake that it is perfect as is, with just a dusting of confectioners' sugar and whipped cream or maybe tart berries on the side.

Serves 8 to 10

❖ FOR THE CRUST

2 cups (240 g) all-purpose flour

½ cup (100 g) granulated sugar

¼ teaspoon salt

⅔ cup (150 g) lightly salted butter, at room temperature

1 large egg, at room temperature

❖ FOR THE FILLING

2 cups (240 g) almonds

2 cups (240 g) confectioners' sugar

3 large egg whites, plus 1 large egg yolk, at room temperature

½ teaspoon vanilla extract

For the crust, in a food processor, pulse together the flour, granulated sugar, salt, and butter until combined. Add the egg and pulse until combined. Transfer the dough to a lightly floured surface and gather it together to form a solid shape. Separate out a third of the dough then roll both pieces into balls and flatten slightly. Wrap each piece of dough in plastic wrap and refrigerate for 30 minutes.

Once the dough has chilled, preheat the oven to 350°F (180°C).

Cut a round piece of parchment paper so it fits perfectly in the bottom of a 9 inch (23 cm) springform pan. Butter the pan, then add the parchment and butter it.

Using your hands, push the larger piece of dough into the bottom and halfway up the sides of the prepared pan. On a lightly floured surface, using a rolling pin and more flour as needed to prevent sticking, roll out the smaller piece dough into a roughly ⅛ inch (3 mm) thick circle. Cut the circle into long even strips for the top of the cake and set aside.

For the filling, in a food processor, pulse together the almonds and confectioners' sugar until finely ground and combined. Transfer to a medium bowl.

In a small bowl, lightly whip the egg whites, then add to the almond mixture, along with the vanilla, and stir until combined. Pour the filling into the prepared crust. Top with the strips of dough, overlapping them to form a lattice pattern.

In a small bowl, whisk the egg yolk with 1 tablespoon of water. Brush onto the pastry lattice and bake for 35 to 45 minutes, or until the crust is golden and the filling has set. Let cool for 10 minutes in the pan, then carefully loosen the sides of the pan and transfer to a wire rack to cool completely. Keep covered in the refrigerator for up to 1 week.

Candied Almond Cake

This classic cake consists of layers of fluffy sponge cake, custard buttercream, and crushed *krokan* — "candied almonds." Bursting with texture and flavor, this is a rich dessert that will take the cake table to a new level. I find this cake gets better after a day or two, when all the flavors have had time to blend together. If making it in advance, wait to cover the cake with the candied almonds until you're ready to serve.

Serves 8 to 10

❖ **FOR THE CAKE**

5 large eggs, at room temperature

½ cup plus 2 tablespoons (125 g) granulated sugar

1 cup (120 g) all-purpose flour

1 teaspoon baking powder

❖ **FOR THE CUSTARD BUTTERCREAM**

¾ cup (170 g) lightly salted butter, at room temperature

1½ cups (180 g) confectioners' sugar

½ cup (100 g) granulated sugar

4 large egg yolks, at room temperature

¼ cup (32 g) cornstarch

2 cups (480 ml) whole milk

½ vanilla bean, split lengthwise, or 1 teaspoon vanilla extract

❖ **FOR THE CANDIED ALMONDS**

1 cup (200 g) granulated sugar

1¾ cups (210 g) almonds, roughly chopped

For the cake, preheat the oven to 350°F (180°C). Cut a round piece of parchment paper so it fits perfectly in the bottom of an 8 inch (20 cm) springform pan. Butter the pan, then add the parchment and butter it.

In a stand mixer fitted with the whisk attachment, whip the eggs and granulated sugar on medium-high for 6 to 8 minutes, or until stiff and light in color. Sift the flour and baking powder over the batter and use a spatula to gently fold until just combined. Pour into the prepared pan and set on a baking sheet. Bake in the middle of the oven for 30 to 35 minutes, or until golden brown. Let cool completely.

For the custard buttercream, in a large bowl, combine the butter and confectioners' sugar. In a second large bowl, whisk together the granulated sugar and egg yolks. Add the cornstarch and whisk until thick and pale yellow.

Put the milk in a small saucepan. Scrape the seeds from the vanilla bean into the milk and add the scraped bean (or add the vanilla extract). Warm over medium heat until just beginning to simmer then remove from the heat. Remove the vanilla bean, then slowly add the milk to the egg yolk mixture, whisking constantly to avoid curdling the eggs. Pour the mixture back into the saucepan and place over medium heat. Cook, stirring constantly, until thick. Let cool completely then combine with the butter and confectioners' sugar mixture. Refrigerate until ready to assemble.

For the candied almonds, line a baking sheet with parchment paper or a silicone mat.

In a large frying pan, melt the granulated sugar over medium heat. Do not stir more than necessary but try to turn the pan gently as the sugar starts to melt. When the sugar is golden and melted, stir in the almonds, then pour the mixture onto the prepared baking sheet, spreading it out as much as possible. Let cool, then break apart into smaller pieces using a knife or a food processor.

To assemble, cut the cake horizontally into 3 even layers. Pour a quarter of the custard buttercream on top of the first layer, then add a sprinkling of the candied almonds. Arrange the second cake layer on top, followed by a quarter of the custard buttercream and a sprinkling of almonds. Top with the final cake layer then cover the top and sides of the cake with the remaining custard buttercream, followed by the remaining almonds. Keep covered in the refrigerator for up to 3 days.

Mini Custard Pies

These delightful shortbread and vanilla custard pies are such a treat, and you'll find them served in bakeries across Norway. It's said they are an extension of *linzer torte*, an Austrian cake, and have been in Norway since at least 1861. These are a joy to make, and you'll end up with leftover custard you can have on the side or use for something else.

Makes 12 individual pies

❖ **FOR THE CUSTARD FILLING**

½ cup (100 g) granulated sugar

4 large egg yolks, at room temperature

3 tablespoons cornstarch

2 cups (480 ml) whole milk

½ vanilla bean, split lengthwise, or 1 teaspoon vanilla extract

❖ **FOR THE SHORTBREAD**

2½ cups (300 g) all-purpose flour

¾ cup plus 1 tablespoon (100 g) confectioners' sugar, plus more for serving

2 teaspoons baking powder

¾ cup (170 g) lightly salted butter, room temperature

1 large egg, at room temperature

For the custard, in a large bowl, whisk together the granulated sugar and egg yolks. Add the cornstarch and whisk until thick and pale yellow.

Put the milk in a small saucepan. Scrape the seeds from the vanilla bean into the milk and add the scraped bean (or add the vanilla extract). Warm over medium heat until just beginning to simmer then remove from the heat. Remove the vanilla bean, then slowly add the milk to the egg yolk mixture, whisking constantly to avoid curdling the eggs. Pour the mixture back into the saucepan and place over medium heat. Cook, stirring constantly, until thick. Set aside to cool.

For the shortbread, in a stand mixer fitted with the paddle attachment, combine the flour, confectioners' sugar, and baking powder. Add the butter and egg and beat to form a soft dough. Cover and refrigerate for 30 minutes.

Once the dough has chilled, preheat the oven to 375°F (190°C). Butter a muffin pan or 12 mini tart pans.

On a lightly floured surface, using a rolling pin and more flour as needed to prevent sticking, roll out two-thirds of the dough until roughly ⅛ inch (3 mm) thick. Using round cookie cutters or a small plate as your guide, cut out 12 circles a little larger than the width of the muffin cups or mini tart pans. Press the circles of dough snuggly into the muffin cups or tart pans. Fill each with a tablespoon or so of custard, leaving some space at the top. Roll out the remaining dough until roughly ⅛ inch (3 mm) thick, then cut out 12 more circles that are roughly the width of the top of the muffin cups or tart pans. Place the circles on top of the custard-filled tarts and press down along the edges to seal. Bake for 20 to 25 minutes, or until golden. Let cool in the pan for 10 minutes before carefully removing and setting on a wire rack. Dust the tops with confectioners' sugar. These are best on the day they are made but will keep covered in the refrigerator for up to 3 days.

Custard and Coconut Buns

These alluring buns, with their flakes of coconut clinging to a sweet glaze and a generous portion of golden custard, are a familiar favorite. *Skoleboller*, translated as "school buns," were placed in children's school lunches as a treat in the 1950s. While no longer confined to the school lunch box, these sweet buns are proudly displayed everywhere and a joy to bake at home. On the last Friday before summer holidays in June, it's customary to eat one or two in celebration.

Makes 12 buns

❖ FOR THE BUNS

1¼ cups (300 ml) lukewarm whole milk

2 large eggs, at room temperature

4 cups (480 g) all-purpose flour

6 tablespoons (75 g) granulated sugar

2 teaspoons (¼ ounce/7 g) instant yeast

2 teaspoons ground cardamon

1¼ teaspoons salt

⅓ cup (75 g) lightly salted butter, cut into small pieces and chilled

❖ FOR THE VANILLA CUSTARD

¼ cup (50 g) granulated sugar

2 large egg yolks, at room temperature

2 tablespoons cornstarch

2 cups (480 ml) whole milk

½ vanilla bean, split lengthwise or 1 teaspoon vanilla extract

❖ FOR THE GLAZE

1 cup (120 g) confectioners' sugar

3 teaspoons egg white

1½ cups (130 g) shredded unsweetened coconut

For the buns, in a small bowl, whisk together the lukewarm milk and 1 of the eggs.

In the bowl of a stand mixer fitted with the dough hook attachment, combine the flour, granulated sugar, yeast, cardamom, and salt. Add the milk mixture and knead on low for 8 minutes. Add the butter and knead on medium for about 5 minutes, or until the dough is very elastic and somewhat moist. Transfer the dough to a lightly buttered bowl, cover with a tea towel, and let rise in a warm spot for about 1 hour, or until doubled in size.

For the custard, in a large bowl, whisk together the granulated sugar and egg yolks (you can save the egg whites for the glaze). Add the cornstarch and whisk until thick and pale yellow.

Put the milk in a small saucepan. Scrape the seeds from the vanilla bean into the milk and add the scraped bean. Warm over medium heat until just beginning to simmer then remove from the heat. Remove the vanilla bean, then slowly add the milk to the egg yolk mixture, whisking constantly to avoid curdling the eggs. Pour the mixture back into the saucepan and place over medium heat. Cook, stirring constantly, until thick. Set aside to cool.

Once the dough has doubled in size, preheat the oven to 425°F (220°C). Line 2 baking sheets with parchment paper.

Divide the dough into 12 equal pieces and use your hands to shape into balls. Place the balls of dough on the prepared baking sheets, cover, and let rise in a warm spot for 30 minutes.

After 30 minutes, using the back of a spoon, make a nice indentation in the center of each ball of dough, pressing down all the way as the dough will spring back. Fill each indentation with 2 to 3 tablespoons of the prepared custard, making sure not to overfill them.   →

In a small bowl, lightly beat the remaining egg. Using a pastry brush, lightly brush the beaten egg on top of the dough. Bake, 1 baking sheet at a time, for 10 to 12 minutes, or until golden brown. Transfer the buns to a wire rack and let cool completely.

For the glaze, in a small bowl, whisk together the confectioners' sugar, egg white, and 3 teaspoons of water to form a somewhat thick glaze. Place the coconut in a wide bowl. Using a spatula, spread the glaze around the custard on top of each bun, then press the glazed area into the coconut so it sticks. Leftover buns can be stored in an airtight bag at room temperature for up to 2 days.

Spelt and Sour Cream Waffles with Spruce Tip Syrup

For a few short weeks in the spring, bright green spruce tips break away from their casings and emerge. We grab our baskets and head into the woods to gather enough to make this delicious syrup, which I also shared in my first cookbook. It has wonderful notes of pine and lemon and will last for the months ahead. While spruce tip syrup is drizzled over many sweet and savory things, waffles are just a brilliant partner. I like pairing it with these spelt and sour cream waffles, because they hold up so well against the syrup, providing a lovely crispy texture with a certain lightness.

If spruce tips or their syrup are hard to get a hold of, you can always serve these waffles on their own or with another fragrant syrup. If you do have access to spruce trees, I recommend making their tips a part of your ingredient repertoire.

Makes 10 waffles

❖ **FOR THE SYRUP**

4¼ cups (1 liter) spruce tips

About 2½ to 3 cups (500 to 600 g) granulated sugar

❖ **FOR THE WAFFLES**

1 cup (240 ml) milk

¾ cup (180 ml) sour cream

4 large eggs, at room temperature

1¼ cups (150 g) white spelt flour

1¼ cups (150 g) all-purpose flour

½ cup (100 g) granulated sugar

⅛ teaspoon salt

½ cup (112 g) lightly salted butter, melted

Whipped cream, for serving

For the syrup, in a medium saucepan, combine the spruce tips with just enough cold water to barley cover them and bring to a boil. Lower the heat and simmer, covered, for 30 minutes. Pour through a mesh strainer into a large, heavy-bottomed saucepan; discard the spruce tips. Measure the liquid and calculate 2 parts sugar for every 3 parts liquid. Combine the calculated sugar and liquid in the large, heavy-bottomed saucepan and bring to a boil. Continue boiling, removing any white foam that forms on top, for 30 to 45 minutes, or until reduced and thickened to the point when the syrup coats the back of a spoon. For accuracy, use a candy thermometer and remove the syrup from the heat when it reaches the thread stage (225°F/110°C). Pour into a clean glass jar, cover with a lid, and let cool completely before using. The syrup will keep in the refrigerator for a couple of months.

For the waffles, in a large bowl, whisk together the milk, sour cream, and eggs. Sift the spelt flour, all-purpose flour, sugar, and salt over the milk mixture and whisk to combine. Let stand for 15 to 20 minutes. Stir in the melted butter.

Heat and butter a waffle iron. Spoon some of the batter onto the iron, close, and bake for 3 to 5 minutes, or until the waffle has the desired texture. Repeat with the remaining batter. Serve warm with whipped cream and the syrup drizzled on top.

Horns with Herby Pea Pesto

Horns are Norway's croissant, but without all the layers of butter or the fuss to make them. In that way, they are closer in nature to a crescent roll. Delicious and versatile, you can fill them with sweet things like chocolate and jam, savory items like cheese and ham, or serve them plain. In the spring, I like to fill horns with a spoonful of my herby pea pesto and some local blue cheese or fresh goat cheese. These are perfect to nibble on in the garden, just as the first of the shoots and buds bloom. Use the dough recipe provided here as your base to explore other variations, too.

Makes 16 horns

❖ FOR THE HORNS

4 cups (480 g) all-purpose flour

4 teaspoons (½ ounce / 14 g) instant yeast

½ teaspoon salt

1⅓ cups (320 ml) milk

½ cup (112 g) lightly salted butter, melted

1 large egg, beaten

Poppy seeds and sesame seeds, for sprinkling

❖ FOR THE FILLING

½ cup (90 g) fresh or frozen peas (defrosted)

½ cup (120 ml) mild-flavored oil

2 garlic cloves

2 teaspoons finely chopped fresh dill

2 teaspoons finely chopped fresh mint

¼ teaspoon salt

Blue cheese or fresh goat cheese

For the horns, in the bowl of a stand mixer fitted with the dough hook attachment, combine the flour, yeast, salt, milk, and melted butter and knead on low for about 10 minutes, or until the dough is soft and pliable. Cover with a tea towel and let rise in a warm spot for about 1 hour, or until doubled in size.

For the filling, in a food processor, combine the peas, oil, garlic, dill, mint, and salt and pulse until combined but still slightly coarse. Set aside.

Once the dough has doubled in size, preheat the oven to 425°F (220°C). Line a baking sheet with parchment paper.

Divide the dough into 2 equal pieces. On a lightly floured surface, using a rolling pin and more flour as needed to prevent sticking, roll out each piece of dough into a large circle, roughly 16 inches (40 cm) in diameter. Using a pizza slicer or knife, cut each dough circle into 8 equal "pizza" slices. Place a spoonful of the pea filling on the wider end of each slice. Place a few blue cheese crumbles or slices of goat cheese on top of the pea filling and roll the dough from the wide end to the narrow end to form a horn or croissant shape. Place the horns, seam side down, on the baking sheet. Brush the tops with the beaten egg and sprinkle with a mixture of poppy and sesame seeds. Bake for 12 to 15 minutes, or until golden brown. Transfer to a wire rack to cool for 5 to 10 minutes before serving. These are best eaten on the day they are baked but will last in an airtight bag at room temperature for up to 2 days.

Creamy Wild Flatbreads

Spring has truly arrived when wild garlic appears and the first of the nettles pop up from the ground. These flatbreads featuring both taste incredible and look amazing—they are a true celebration of nature. Plan to make the marinated mushrooms a few hours in advance and double the recipe if there are more mouths to feed. You can always substitute garlic chives for the wild garlic and spinach for the nettles if you can't access them.

Serves 4

❖ **FOR THE MARINATED MUSHROOMS**

3 tablespoons olive oil

7 ounces (200 g) mixed mushrooms, sliced

1 small garlic clove, crushed

1½ tablespoons apple cider vinegar

½ teaspoon granulated sugar

⅛ teaspoon salt

Pinch of freshly ground black pepper

❖ **FOR THE FLATBREADS**

2 cups (240 g) all-purpose flour

1 teaspoon (⅛ ounce / 3.5 g) instant yeast

1 teaspoon salt

⅔ cup (160 ml) lukewarm water

3 tablespoons mild-flavored oil

❖ **FOR THE NETTLE SAUCE**

Small handful of nettle leaves

½ cup (120 ml) heavy cream

1 garlic clove

¼ teaspoon salt

For the marinated mushrooms, in a large skillet, heat 1 tablespoon of the olive oil over medium-high heat. Add the mushrooms and sauté for 8 to 10 minutes, or until the mushrooms have released most of their moisture.

In a medium bowl, combine the remaining 2 tablespoons of olive oil with the garlic, vinegar, sugar, salt, and pepper. Add the cooked mushrooms and stir to combine. Cover and refrigerate for at least 4 hours.

For the flatbreads, in the bowl of a stand mixer fitted with the dough hook attachment, combine the flour, yeast, and salt. Add the lukewarm water and mild-flavored oil and knead on low for about 5 minutes, or until the dough is soft and pliable. Transfer to a lightly buttered bowl, cover with a tea towel, and let rise in a warm spot for about 1 hour, or until doubled in size.

For the nettle sauce, bring a small saucepan of cold water to a boil. Add the nettles and simmer for 30 to 60 seconds. Drain and rinse under running cold water. Squeeze out all the excess liquid from the nettles. Set aside a couple of nettle leaves to go on top of the flatbreads. Transfer the rest of the blanched nettles to a food processor. Add the heavy cream, garlic, and salt and pulse until the mixture begins to thicken, 30 seconds to 1 minute. Transfer the sauce to a bowl. Clean and wipe down the food processor to make the wild garlic sauce.

For the wild garlic sauce, in the food processor, combine the heavy cream, salt, and most of the wild garlic—set aside a few leaves to go on top of the flatbreads—and pulse until the mixture begins to thicken, 30 seconds to 1 minute.

Once the dough has doubled in size, preheat the oven to 475°F (240°C). Line 2 baking sheets with parchment paper.   →

❖ **FOR THE WILD GARLIC SAUCE**

½ cup (120 ml) heavy cream

¼ teaspoon salt

1 ounce (28 g) wild garlic leaves

❖ **TO FINISH**

3 ½ ounces (100 g) fresh goat's
   cheese

Couple of slices Gruyère

Honey, for serving

Divide the dough into 4 equal pieces. On a lightly floured surface, using a rolling pin and more flour as needed to prevent sticking, roll out each piece of dough into an oblong shape that measures roughly 12 x 6 inches (30 x 15 cm).

Arrange the flatbreads on the prepared baking sheets. Spread the nettle sauce on 2 of the flatbreads and spread wild garlic sauce on the other 2 flatbreads. Sprinkle the goat's cheese and arrange a couple slices of Gruyère on top of each flatbread. Add the marinated mushrooms and the blanched nettle leaves to the flatbreads with the nettle sauce. Add some fresh wild garlic leaves to the flatbreads with the wild garlic sauce. Bake, 1 baking sheet at a time, for 6 to 8 minutes, or until the tops are bubbling and the flatbreads are golden. Drizzle honey on the wild garlic flatbreads and serve immediately.

Nettle Milk Almond Tart

Each bite of this tart tastes as if the clouds are touching the earth. Nettles are a superfood and have a wonderful earthy flavor, and this sweet tart doesn't shy away from letting that shine. I like to gather fresh nettles when they start appearing in the spring and air dry them in a cool, dark spot. Once dry, I grind them into a fine powder. You can easily dry your own nettles at home if you have them readily available. Alternatively, nettle powder can be found at farmers' markets, specialty shops, and online.

Serves 8

❖ FOR THE TART

1¾ cups (210 g) all-purpose flour

½ cup (50 g) almond flour

½ cup (60 g) confectioners' sugar

½ cup (112 g) lightly salted butter, cut into pieces and chilled

1 large egg, at room temperature

❖ FOR THE NETTLE CUSTARD

½ cup (100 g) granulated sugar

¼ cup (32 g) cornstarch

1 tablespoon nettle powder, plus more for serving

¼ teaspoon salt

3 large egg yolks, at room temperature

2 cups (480 ml) whole milk

❖ FOR THE WHIPPED CREAM

2 cups (480 ml) heavy cream

2½ tablespoons confectioners' sugar

For the tart, preheat the oven to 350°F (180°C).

In a food processor, combine the all-purpose flour, almond flour, and confectioners' sugar. Add the butter and pulse. With the machine running, add the egg to form a dough.

On a lightly floured surface, using a rolling pin and more flour as needed to prevent sticking, roll out the dough into a 13 inch (33 cm) circle. Carefully lay the dough evenly over an 11 inch (28 cm) round tart pan with a removable base and press it to fit with your hands. Using a fork, prick holes over the base of the dough and refrigerate for 30 minutes.

Once the dough has chilled, remove from the refrigerator and bake for about 20 minutes, or until just turning golden. Let cool completely in the pan.

For the custard, in a large bowl, whisk together the granulated sugar, cornstarch, nettle powder, and salt.

Whisk in the egg yolks. In a small saucepan, warm the milk over low heat until just beginning to simmer then remove from the heat. Slowly add the milk to the egg yolk mixture, whisking constantly to avoid curdling the eggs. Pour the mixture back into the saucepan and place over medium heat. Cook, stirring constantly, until thick. Pour into the cooled tart. Cover the top of the custard with plastic wrap, gently pressing the plastic directly onto the custard to prevent a skin from forming, then refrigerate for about 3 hours, or until set.

For the whipped cream, in a large bowl, whip the heavy cream and confectioners' sugar until stiff peaks form.

When ready to serve, cover the chilled tart with the whipped cream and dust with nettle powder. Carefully remove the rim of the pan by gently pressing upwards on the bottom of the pan while holding the rim in place. Transfer the tart to a serving plate. Keep covered in the refrigerator for up to 3 days.

Dandelion Petal Honey Shortbreads

When the flowers have popped up in the fields and the bees are buzzing around, I look forward to acquiring some local honey, knowing the flavors will draw me straight to where the bees have been dancing. A simple honey on toast will do on most days, but for afternoons in the garden, it's nice to have a little treat. Shortbreads are delicate and flaky but still rich and buttery. When you add honey and sweet dandelion petals, the flavors become more nuanced and robust, while the specks of petals are a gorgeous reminder of the season.

It took me many years to appreciate dandelions for the superfood they are and see beyond their "weed" label. As children, we would rejoice in blowing their pappi in the gentle breeze, as though a troupe of dancers were swirling in the sky, destinations to be seen. It was magical, but as fun as it was to blow the wispy seeds as we made wishes, someone was always there to remind us that we were only helping to spread these vicious weeds. As the years passed, I barely gave them a second thought. How wrong I was. I hope these cookies inspire you to start using dandelions in your kitchen.

Makes 16 cookies

¾ cup (170 g) lightly salted butter, at room temperature

⅓ cup (65 g) granulated sugar, plus more for finishing

¼ cup (60 ml) honey, plus more for brushing

1½ cups (180 g) all-purpose flour

½ cup plus 1 tablespoon (75 g) cornstarch

¼ teaspoon salt

½ cup (8 g) dandelion petals, yellow parts only

Preheat the oven to 340°F (170°C). Line a baking sheet with parchment paper.

In the bowl of a stand mixer fitted with the paddle attachment, beat the butter, sugar, and honey until light and fluffy. Add the flour, cornstarch, and salt and blend to form a soft dough. Gently fold in the dandelion petals. Wrap the dough in plastic wrap and refrigerate for 30 minutes.

Once the dough has chilled, place it on a lightly floured surface. Using a rolling pin and more flour as needed to prevent sticking, roll out the dough into a 9 ½ inch (24 cm) square. Cut the square in half and then cut it in the opposite direction into 16 equal strips. Place the shortbreads on the prepared baking sheet.

Warm a few tablespoons of honey. Use a pastry brush to brush the tops of the cookies with the warm honey, then sprinkle with a little sugar. Bake for 20 to 25 minutes, or until golden brown on top. Cool on a wire rack before serving. These cookies will last a couple of days in an airtight container at room temperature.

Simple Rhubarb Cake

There's that moment in late spring when the rhubarb plants begin to bud and soon after the leaves unravel and expand, revealing long stalks in shades of bright pink, deep crimson, and earthy green. It's the culmination of a year-long wait to enjoy a fresh stalk dipped in sugar, while filling a basket to then make homemade pies, bowls of sweet soup, warm crumbles, pitchers of fresh juice and, of course, this simple and fluffy cake.

When you bite into this cake, you taste the delicate sponge, with a bit of tang from the rhubarb, and then a delightful crunch from the sugar and almonds on top. So simple and yet so good.

Serves 8 to 10

¾ cup (150 g) granulated sugar,
   plus more for sprinkling

⅔ cup (150 g) lightly salted butter,
   at room temperature

2 large eggs, at room temperature

1½ cups (180 g) all-purpose flour

1½ teaspoons baking powder

½ cup (120 ml) whole milk

½ pound (225 g) rhubarb, cut into
   ½ inch (1.25 cm) pieces

2 tablespoons sliced almonds

Whipped cream or ice cream,
   for serving

Preheat the oven to 350°F (180°C). Butter an 8 inch (20 cm) springform pan.

In the bowl of a stand mixer fitted with the paddle attachment, beat the sugar and butter until light and fluffy. Add the eggs, 1 at a time, incorporating each egg before adding the next, and beat until light and creamy. Add the flour, baking powder, and milk and beat until well blended. Pour the batter into the prepared pan. Place the rhubarb pieces on top of the batter, arranging them in concentric circles and gently pressing them into the batter. Sprinkle with the sliced almonds and about 2 tablespoons of sugar. Bake for 35 to 40 minutes, or until a toothpick inserted in the center comes out clean and the top of the cake is golden brown. Cool slightly in the pan before serving with whipped cream or ice cream. Keep covered in the refrigerator for up to 4 days.

Midnight Sun

❖   Midnattssol

❖ **TIME GETS LOST IN THE LIGHT.** It's hard to distinguish between the hours when the sun never fully sets, hovering low at midnight, while casting its magical glow across the landscape. It's the charm of the *midnattssol*, "midnight sun," that enchants and entices. This natural phenomenon, occurring in northern Norway, lures and tempts with its proclamation of eternal daylight.

Summer in Norway is antithetical to its winter. It's when the light shines bright, engulfing the whole space and not letting go, making up for lost time. Months of hibernation lead to spending hours awake, long into the night, to soak it all in. The summer solstice, or longest day of the year, is marked by Midsummer and bonfires across the land are lit in celebration. Bright berries, tantalizing fruits, aromatic herbs, and mouthwatering vegetables make their debut, as gardens and meadows flourish. Wild edibles and garden plants marry perfectly together. Meals are more often than not enjoyed outdoors, and the kitchen is met with a vibrancy of choice. Baking becomes a kaleidoscope of flavors—mirroring nature—and our bellies are filled with the joys that the light touches.

Rhubarb and Rose Napoleon Cake

Napoleonskake, a common pastry you'll find all over Norway, features a thick layer of vanilla cream, perfectly buoyant thanks to gelatin, and sandwiched between two thin layers of pastry. This version is more relaxed and flavored with tangy rhubarb and floral notes. The cream is soft, the layers are thick, and it's all a bit messy when it comes down to cutting it, but it's sure beautiful and tasty. You can make your own rose water by infusing fresh, organic rose petals in simmering water. You can also make everything a day in advance and assemble when ready to serve.

Serves 6

❖ **FOR THE PUFF PASTRY**

2 cups (240 g) all-purpose flour

¼ teaspoon salt

½ cup (120 ml) ice water

1 cup (224 g) lightly salted butter, chilled

❖ **FOR THE COMPOTE**

4 cups (450 g) rhubarb, cleaned and cut into bite size pieces

¾ cup (150 g) granulated sugar

1 teaspoon rose water

❖ **FOR THE VANILLA CREAM**

¼ cup (50 g) granulated sugar

4 large egg yolks, at room temperature

¼ cup (32 g) cornstarch

1¾ cups (420 ml) whole milk

½ vanilla bean, split lengthwise, or 1 teaspoon vanilla extract

⅔ cup (160 ml) heavy cream

❖ **FOR THE ROSE GLAZE**

½ cup plus 2 tablespoons (75 g) confectioners' sugar

1½ teaspoons rose water

For the puff pastry, in a medium bowl, whisk together the flour and salt. Transfer the mixture to a clean surface and make a well in the center. Add a little of the ice water to the well and, using your hands or a fork, gently toss with the flour mixture. Continue adding the rest of the water until the dough comes together, adding more water as needed. Press the dough into a square, wrap in plastic wrap, and refrigerate for at least 30 minutes.

Place the butter between 2 sheets of parchment paper. Using a rolling pin, pound the butter gently to flatten and soften it. Fold the butter on to itself and continue pounding until quite pliable. Shape the butter into a 5 inch (12.5 cm) square, wrap in plastic wrap, and refrigerate for at least 30 minutes.

Once the dough has chilled, place it on a lightly floured surface. Using a rolling pin and more flour as needed to prevent sticking, roll out the dough into a square large enough for the butter to fit in the center with a 3 inch (7.5 cm) border. Place the butter in the center and wrap the dough around it, overlapping the dough and pinching the edges to seal. Turn the dough over, so the folded side sits directly on the lightly floured surface. Flour the rolling pin and roll out the dough into a long rectangle. Fold the top one-third of the rectangle down to the center, then fold the bottom one-third up and over that, like you would fold a letter. Rotate the dough a quarter turn and roll out into another long rectangle. Fold like a letter as before then wrap in plastic wrap and refrigerate for 30 minutes. This is 2 turns.

Repeat the rolling out, folding, and chilling process 2 more times for a total of 6 turns. If you notice any butter coming through the dough, pat it with a little flour. Wrap in plastic wrap and refrigerate at least 30 minutes.

Preheat the oven to 400°F (200°C). Line 2 baking sheets with parchment paper.

On a lightly floured surface, using a rolling pin and more flour as needed to prevent sticking, roll out the dough into a large rectangle that measures roughly 24 x 8 inches (60 x 20 cm) with the long sides horizontal.   →

Cut the dough crosswise into 6 equal portions, each measuring about 8 x 4 inches (20 x 10 cm). Transfer the dough to the parchment-lined baking sheets. Use a fork to poke holes across the dough to prevent it from bubbling up. Bake, 1 baking sheet at a time, for about 15 minutes, or until golden. Transfer to a wire rack to cool. If puffy, gently press down on the pastries to flatten them slightly.

For the compote, in a medium saucepan, bring the rhubarb and granulated sugar to a simmer. Continue simmering for about 15 minutes, or until the mixture has thickened and the rhubarb has broken down. Add the rose water. Set aside to cool.

For the custard, in a large bowl, whisk together the granulated sugar and egg yolks. Add the cornstarch and whisk until thick and pale yellow.

Put the milk in a small saucepan. Scrape the seeds from the vanilla bean into the milk and add the scraped bean. Warm over medium heat until just beginning to simmer then remove from the heat. Remove the vanilla bean, then slowly add the milk to the egg yolk mixture, whisking constantly to avoid curdling the eggs. Pour the mixture back into the saucepan and place over medium heat. Cook, stirring constantly, until thick. Set aside to cool.

Whip the heavy cream until stiff peaks form and gently fold into the cooled custard.

For the glaze, in a small bowl, whisk together the confectioners' sugar, rose water, and ½ tablespoon of water until smooth and combined.

To assemble, place 2 of the pastries on a serving platter and spread a quarter of the rhubarb compote on top of each. Add a good amount of the custard then top with a second layer of pastry. Divide the remaining compote between the pastries and top with more custard—you might have some leftovers. Add the final layer of pastry then spread the glaze on top. To make it easier to cut, chill in the refrigerator before serving. Keep covered in the refrigerator for up to 3 days.

Viking Pizza with Wild Strawberries, Cured Pork, and Honey

It's undeniable how popular pizza is in Norway today, but findings show that Norwegians were baking their own variety—known as *brødtallerken* ("bread-dish") and nicknamed "Viking pizza"—since ancient times. The bread would have been cooked on flat, round metal pans with long handles and propped over the fire. Made with barley or rye flour, it's possible this dish was the main grain-based food eaten daily. Just like pizza, the bread would have been topped with ingredients that were readily available, such as cheese, cured meats, fish, and wild bird eggs. In the summer, when succulent wild strawberries are ripe and we have an abundance of honey, cured meats, and cheeses from the summer farms, I jump at the opportunity to make this pizza. It's sweet, savory, and ridiculously good—the kind of meal a Viking or anyone else would certainly enjoy with a cold glass of beer or mead.

Makes four 12 inch (30 cm) pizzas

❖ FOR THE DOUGH

1½ cups (360 ml) lukewarm water

½ tablespoon granulated sugar

2 teaspoons (¼ ounce / 7 g) active dry yeast

¾ cup (90 g) barley flour

3⅓ cups (400 g) all-purpose flour

½ tablespoon salt

2 tablespoons mild-flavored oil

❖ FOR THE TOPPING

Semi-aged goat's cheese, sliced

Thinly sliced cured pork

Handful of wild strawberries

Runny summer honey

For the dough, in a small bowl, combine the lukewarm water and sugar, stirring to dissolve the sugar. Add the yeast and stir until combined. Let sit for about 5 minutes, or until foamy.

In the bowl of a stand mixer fitted with the dough hook attachment, combine the barley flour, all-purpose flour, and salt. Add the yeast mixture and 1 tablespoon of the oil and knead on medium-low for 8 minutes. Transfer the dough to a large bowl coated with the remaining 1 tablespoon of oil, cover with a tea towel, and let rise in a warm spot for about 1 hour, or until doubled in size.

Once the dough has double in size, preheat a pizza oven or regular oven to 450°F (230°C).

Transfer the dough to a lightly floured surface and divide into 4 equal pieces. Use your hands to stretch out each piece of dough into a 12 inch (30 cm) pizza base.

For the topping, place a couple slices of the goat's cheese on top of each base, followed by slices of the cured pork. Bake in a pizza oven, turning the dough a few times, for about 1 ½ minutes, or until golden brown. If using a regular oven, place on a baking sheet or pizza stone, and cook for about 8 minutes, or until golden brown. Repeat until all the pizzas are cooked. To serve, top with the fresh wild strawberries and a good drizzle of honey.

Strawberry "Snipper" Shortcakes

Snipper were one of the first treats I tasted when we moved to our current home in the valley of Numedal. These soft and pillow-like cookies are shaped like diamonds and everyone has their own recipe. I wanted to play around with the traditional version and ended up combining it with one of my favorite summer treats, strawberry shortcake. In place of a biscuit, I use snipper dough, and rather than shaping it into diamonds, my cookies are round. Ripe strawberries, bursting with sweetness, are nestled inside and on top, along with whipped cream, for a dreamy summer treat. You'll want to assemble these when you're ready to serve them.

Makes 10 to 12 shortcakes

❖ FOR THE STRAWBERRIES

2.2 pounds (1 kg) hulled
   strawberries, sliced

½ cup (100 g) granulated sugar

❖ FOR THE SHORTCAKES

½ cup plus 1 tablespoon (125 g)
   lightly salted butter

1 cup (240 ml) kefir or buttermilk

3¾ cups (450 g) all-purpose flour

1 cup (200 g) granulated sugar,
   plus more for sprinkling

1½ teaspoons ground cardamom

1½ teaspoons baking powder

Milk, for finishing

❖ FOR THE WHIPPED CREAM

1¼ cups (300 ml) heavy cream

For the strawberries, in a medium bowl, combine the strawberries and sugar. Set aside to allow the juices to release while you make the shortcakes.

For the shortcakes, preheat the oven to 400°F (200°C). Line a baking sheet with parchment paper.

In a small saucepan, melt the butter over low heat. Pour the butter into a small bowl and stir in the kefir.

In a large bowl, whisk together the flour, sugar, cardamom, and baking powder. Add the butter mixture and combine until you get a firm and smooth dough.

On a well-floured surface, turn out the dough and use your hands to flatten until about ½ inch (1.25 cm) thick. Using a 3 inch (7.5 cm) round cookie cutter or the rim of a glass, cut the dough into circles, re-rolling any scraps to make 10 to 12 shortcakes. Place them on the prepared baking sheet, brush the tops with milk, and sprinkle with sugar. Bake for 10 to 12 minutes, or until light golden. Transfer to a wire rack and let cool for 15 minutes before assembling.

For the whipped cream, in a medium bowl, whip the cream until stiff peaks form.

To serve, cut the shortcakes horizontally in half. Place the bottom halves on a tray, cut side facing up, and spoon half of the strawberries and their juices on top, followed by half of the whipped cream. Top with the remaining shortcake halves and spoon the remaining berries and whipped cream on top. Serve immediately.

Thin Pancakes with Strawberries and Brown Cheese Caramel

Summer is all about succulent strawberries and we have some of the best in Norway. The cooler climate gives the berries the time to ripen slowly, becoming juicier and sweeter with each day. These pancakes couple that fresh sweetness with a caramel sauce made with traditional brown cheese. It's a nod to the Norwegian summer farms where brown cheese, fresh fruit jams, and flat cakes — similar to griddle cakes — are staples. To get nicely browned and bubbly pancakes, cook over a higher heat and add butter every time.

Serves 4 to 6

❖ FOR THE PANCAKES

¾ cup (90 g) whole wheat flour

¾ cup (90 g) all-purpose flour

½ teaspoon salt

2 cups plus 1 tablespoon
    plus 1 teaspoon (500 ml) milk

4 large eggs, at room temperature

Butter, for frying

❖ FOR THE STRAWBERRIES

5½ cups (735 g) hulled
    strawberries, cut into smaller
    pieces

1 tablespoon honey

❖ FOR THE CARAMEL SAUCE

3½ ounces (100 g) Norwegian
    brown cheese, sliced or grated

½ cup (120 ml) heavy cream

½ cup (100 g) granulated sugar

For the pancakes, in a large bowl, whisk together the whole wheat flour, all-purpose flour, and salt. Slowly pour in the milk, a little at a time, until you have a smooth batter without any lumps. Add the eggs and mix well to combine. Let stand for 15 to 20 minutes.

For the strawberries, in a small saucepan, bring 3 cups (400 g) of the strawberries and the honey to a simmer over medium-high heat. Continue simmering for about 10 minutes, or until the strawberries are soft and the sauce is slightly thick. Set aside to cool.

For the caramel sauce, in another small saucepan, bring the brown cheese, heavy cream, and sugar to a simmer over medium-high heat. Continue simmering, whisking frequently, for 5 to 8 minutes, or until fully combined and thickened to a caramel sauce consistency — somewhat thick but still a little runny. Set aside.

In a large frying pan, melt some butter over medium-high heat. Ladle in about ½ cup (120 ml) of the pancake batter, moving the pan around to coat the bottom evenly with the batter. Cook for about 30 seconds, or until the bottom of the pancake has set and turned golden brown. Flip the pancake and cook for about 30 seconds more, or until the other side is golden brown. Transfer the pancake to a plate and cover with foil to keep warm. Add more butter to the pan and continue this process until all the batter has been used up. You should get 8 to 10 pancakes.

To serve, drizzle some of the brown cheese caramel sauce on top of each pancake, followed by the strawberry sauce and the remaining fresh strawberry pieces. Store leftover pancakes covered in the refrigerator for up to 2 days.

Meadowsweet Cheesecake

The summer fields are full of *mjødurt*—"meadowsweet"—in full bloom, permeating the air with the sweet scent of floral almonds. Creamy white clusters of flowers atop tall stems nestle in among the green grasses and wildflowers, creating a beautiful sight for the eyes. I like to use the flowers to infuse the cream for this baked cheesecake. It has an alluring taste of almond, with hints of hay and vanilla, that is perfect to indulge in, just as the day is cooling off and the sun is lowering down.

As with any wild edible, you need to be 100 percent sure you have identified the correct plant. A good substitute for meadowsweet would be elderflower, but it will provide a fruity and floral taste rather than a punch of aromatic almond tones. Plan to make this a day ahead.

Serves 8 to 10

❖ FOR THE MEADOWSWEET CREAM

1½ cups (360 ml) heavy cream

20 meadowsweet blossoms in bloom, plus a few more blossoms for decorating

❖ FOR THE CHEESECAKE

8 ounces (225 g) whole wheat digestive biscuits, roughly crushed

½ cup (112 g) lightly salted butter, melted

17½ ounces (500 g) cream cheese

1 cup (200 g) granulated sugar

2 large eggs, at room temperature

1 teaspoon vanilla extract

1 cup (240 ml) meadowsweet cream

2 tablespoons all-purpose flour

½ teaspoon salt

For the meadowsweet cream, combine the heavy cream and meadowsweet blossoms in a glass container and place in the refrigerator to infuse overnight. Using a fine-mesh strainer, strain the cream into a clean container and discard the blossoms.

For the cheesecake, preheat the oven to 400°F (200°C). Butter a 10 inch (25 cm) springform pan, then line with 2 overlapping sheets of parchment paper, so the parchment is 2 inches (5 cm) above the top of the pan on all sides. There will be creases in the parchment paper, so the resulting edge of the cheesecake will not be smooth.

In a large bowl, stir together the biscuits and melted butter. Press the biscuit mixture evenly into the bottom of the prepared pan.

In the bowl of a stand mixer fitted with the paddle attachment, blend together the cream cheese and sugar, scraping down the sides of the bowl as necessary, for about 30 seconds, or until smooth. Add the eggs, 1 at a time, incorporating each egg before adding the next. Add the vanilla and 1 cup (240 ml) of the meadowsweet cream (leftover cream can be used to flavor coffee or tea), and beat, scraping down the sides of the bowl as necessary, until incorporated. Add the flour and salt and blend until combined. Pour the batter into the biscuit crust. Bake for about 60 minutes, or until golden brown on top and jiggly in the center (it will set while cooling). Cool in the pan for 1 hour.

To serve, decorate the top of the cheesecake with meadowsweet blossoms and serve warm, or refrigerate to chill and firm up even more. Keep covered in the refrigerator for up to 5 days.

Farmhouse Cheese and Sour Cherry Tart

Sour cherries are the kind of cherries you want to bake with, begging to be turned into delicious things like this rustic tart. In the summer, I'll often make batches of this simple farmhouse cheese to adorn the table next to other offerings for our breads and crackers. But when the sour cherries on our trees are ripe, I'll make a batch specifically for this. The pairing of buttery pastry, soft cheese, and sweetened tangy cherries will convert anyone over to the sour side.

Serves 8 to 10

❖ **FOR THE FARMHOUSE CHEESE**
6¼ cups (1.5 liters) whole milk
2 cups plus 1 tablespoon plus
  1 teaspoon (500 ml) buttermilk

❖ **FOR THE COMPOTE**
3 cups (500 g) sour cherries, pitted
½ cup (100 g) granulated sugar

❖ **FOR THE PASTRY**
⅔ cup (150 g) lightly salted butter,
  at room temperature
½ cup (100 g) granulated sugar
1 large egg, at room temperature
1 large egg yolk, at room
  temperature
2½ cups (300 g) all-purpose flour
Pinch of salt
Confectioners' sugar, for serving

For the farmhouse cheese, in a large, heavy-bottomed pot, warm the milk and buttermilk over medium-high heat, stirring often, until the curds and whey begin to separate. Remove from the heat and let stand for 5 minutes. Using a slotted spoon, transfer the curds to a cheesecloth-lined colander set over a bowl. Gather up the cheesecloth and squeeze any excess whey into the colander set over a large bowl. Save the whey for another use.

For the cherry compote, in a medium saucepan, cook the cherries and granulated sugar over medium-high heat for 15 to 20 minutes, or until thickened.

For the pastry, in the bowl of a stand mixer fitted with the paddle attachment, beat the butter and granulated sugar until light and fluffy. Add the egg, egg yolk, flour, and salt and beat until combined. Refrigerate for 30 minutes.

Place a baking sheet in the center of the oven and preheat the oven to 350°F (180°C). Butter a 9 inch (23 cm) springform pan.

On a lightly floured surface, using a rolling pin and more flour as needed to prevent sticking, roll out two-thirds of the dough into a 12 inch (30 cm) circle. Press the dough into the bottom and up the sides of the prepared pan. Spread the cherry compote evenly on top of the dough, then top with the farmhouse cheese.

Roll out the remaining dough into a roughly ⅛ inch (3 mm) thick circle and cut into ¾ inch (2 cm) strips to fit on top of the tart. Arrange the dough strips in an overlapping lattice pattern on top of the filling, pressing firmly on the edges to seal.

Place the tart on the rimmed baking sheet and bake for 40 to 45 minutes, or until golden. Cool completely in the pan before transferring to a serving plate. Dust with confectioners' sugar and serve. Store leftovers covered in the refrigerator for up to 4 days.

Sour Cherry Crisp with Almonds and Seeds

When the slender tree branches are laden with luscious dark cherries, it's time to relieve them of their seasonal burden. As always, it's on a first come first serve basis: us or the birds. Walking through an orchard teeming full of berry bushes and fruit trees, I can't help but recount all the times my friends and I would use the garden as our own playground when we were little. We would pluck fruit from the trees in such earnest that our hands would be stained, the lower parts of our shirts would become makeshift baskets, our conversations were limited as we kept our mouths full of our succulent findings, and our greediness was shown outright, as we left with full bellies and as much fruit as we could carry. That feeling of excitement never leaves, though now I have a little more restraint, thanks to being older and a bit wiser.

One of the most gratifying desserts I like to make with the first cherries of the season is an old-fashioned crisp. The topping needs to be full of nuts and seeds, a nod to *knekkebrød*, "crisp breads," which have the texture and heartiness to match up against those delicious sour cherries. You can always swap out the cherries for plums, apples, and currants, or mix and match with what's in season.

Serves 6 to 8

❖ FOR THE FILLING

2 pounds (900 g) sour cherries, pitted

½ cup (100 g) granulated sugar

3 tablespoons cornstarch

❖ FOR THE TOPPING

½ cup (60 g) all-purpose flour

⅔ cup (66 g) rolled oats

⅔ cup (108 g) dark brown sugar

⅛ teaspoon salt

6 tablespoons (84 g) lightly salted butter, chilled

3 tablespoons sliced almonds

2 tablespoons pumpkin seeds

1 tablespoon flax seeds

1 tablespoon sesame seeds

Whipped cream or vanilla ice cream, for serving

Preheat the oven to 375°F (190°C). Butter a 9 inch (23 cm) pie dish.

For the filling, in a large bowl, combine the cherries, granulated sugar, and cornstarch. Pour into the prepared dish.

For the topping, in a large bowl, whisk together the flour, oats, brown sugar, and salt. Using a pastry cutter or your hands, cut in the butter until the mixture is crumbly. Fold in the almonds, pumpkin seeds, flax seeds, and sesame seeds until combined. Sprinkle the topping evenly over the cherry mixture. Bake for 30 to 35 minutes, or until bubbling on the sides and golden brown on top. Let cool slightly before serving with whipped cream or vanilla ice cream. Store leftovers covered in the refrigerator for up to 5 days.

Raspberry and Red Currant Jam-Filled Doughnuts

Our red currant bushes come to life at the same time the raspberry bushes do, so when we have an overabundance, I make a simple jam with both. It's beautifully tart and sweet at the same time, which is why I use it to fill our *berlinerboller*—fried doughnuts rolled in sugar. I prefer to leave the seeds in the jam, as I like the texture, but you can strain them out if you please. These are the best eaten the day they are made.

Makes 15 large doughnuts

❖ FOR THE JAM

17½ ounces (500 g) raspberries

4 ounces (112 g) red currants

1¾ cups plus 2 tablespoons (375 g) granulated sugar

Juice of ½ lemon

❖ FOR THE DOUGHNUTS

4½ cups (540 g) all-purpose flour

⅓ cup (65 g) granulated sugar, plus more for coating

2 teaspoons (¼ ounce / 7 g) instant yeast

1 teaspoon ground cardamom

½ teaspoon salt

1¼ cups (300 ml) lukewarm whole milk

2 large eggs, at room temperature

6 tablespoons (84 g) lightly salted butter, cubed and chilled

6¼ cups (1 ½ liters) canola or vegetable oil, for frying

For the jam, in a large, heavy-bottomed saucepan, bring the raspberries, red currants, sugar, and lemon juice to a boil. Continue boiling, stirring frequently and skimming off any foam from the top, for about 10 minutes, or until reduced by half. Remove from the stove and let cool.

For the doughnuts, in the bowl a stand mixer fitted with the dough hook attachment, combine the flour, sugar, yeast, cardamom, and salt. Add the lukewarm milk and eggs and knead on low for 10 minutes. Add the butter and knead for 8 minutes, or until the dough is smooth and elastic. Transfer the dough to a lightly buttered bowl, cover with a tea towel, and let rise in a warm spot for about 1 hour, or until doubled in size.

Once the dough has doubled in size, place on a lightly floured surface. Using a rolling pin and more flour as needed to prevent sticking, roll the dough out to a thickness of ½ inch (1.25 cm). Using a 3 inch (7.5 cm) round cookie cutter, cut circles out of the dough. Reroll any scraps and continue the process until all the dough is used up and you have roughly 15 circles of dough. Cover the dough with a tea towel and let rise for 30 minutes.

In a large, heavy-bottomed saucepan, heat the canola or vegetable oil to 350°F (180°C).

Line a large plate with paper towels. Place some sugar in a bowl.

Carefully place 3 to 4 doughnuts in the oil and fry, turning once, about 2 minutes per side, or until golden brown on both sides. Transfer to the paper towel-lined plate and cool for 30 seconds before rolling in the sugar. Repeat with the remaining dough.

Fill a piping bag with the jam. Poke a hole in the side of each doughnut and pipe the jam into the holes. Serve immediately.

Boozy "Black and Blue" Berry Layered Cake

This is my kind of cake. You can serve it for friends in the garden or as the centerpiece at a wedding. It's elegant and complex but not overly fussy. Norwegian gin is some of the best and I like to marry it with dark summer berries. It doesn't overwhelm, just lingers subtly. You can, of course, leave it out. Either way, summer is a little brighter with these berries and buttercream nestled into vanilla layers.

Serves 12 to 16

❖ **FOR THE CAKE**

4 cups (480 g) all-purpose flour

2 teaspoons baking powder

1 teaspoon baking soda

1 teaspoon salt

1½ cups (360 ml) buttermilk

1 cup (240 ml) mild-flavored oil

2 cups (400 g) granulated sugar

1 tablespoon vanilla extract

4 large eggs, at room temperature

❖ **FOR THE BLACKBERRY AND BLUEBERRY COMPOTE**

1½ cups (190 g) blackberries, plus more for serving

1½ cups (190 g) blueberries, plus more for serving

¼ cup (60 ml) honey

2 tablespoons gin (optional)

❖ **FOR THE BUTTERCREAM**

1 cup (224 g) lightly salted butter, at room temperature

3 cups (360 g) confectioners' sugar

3 tablespoons heavy cream

1 teaspoon vanilla extract

For the cake, preheat the oven to 350°F (180°C). Cut 2 round pieces of parchment paper, so they fit perfectly in the bottom of two 8 inch (20 cm) springform pans. Butter the pans then add the parchment paper and butter it.

In a medium bowl, whisk together the flour, baking powder, baking soda, and salt.

In the bowl of a stand mixer fitted with the paddle attachment, beat together the buttermilk, oil, granulated sugar, and vanilla. Add the eggs, 1 at a time, incorporating each egg before adding the next, and beat for about 3 minutes, or until light and creamy. Add the flour mixture and beat until just combined. Divide the batter between the 2 prepared cake pans. Bake for 30 to 40 minutes, or until a toothpick inserted in the center comes out clean. Cool slightly in the pans before transferring to a wire rack to cool completely.

For the blackberry and blueberry compote, in a medium saucepan, bring the blackberries, blueberries, and honey to a simmer over medium-high heat. Continue simmering for 8 to 10 minutes, or until thickened and reduced by half. Stir in the gin, if using. Set aside to cool.

For the buttercream, in the bowl of a stand mixer fitted with the paddle attachment, beat the butter and confectioners' sugar until light and fluffy. Add the heavy cream and vanilla and blend until smooth.

To assemble, cut each cake horizontally in half. Place 1 cake layer on a serving plate. Spread a thin layer of buttercream over the bottom layer, followed by a third of the compote. Arrange the second cake layer on top and repeat the process of adding the buttercream and compote. Arrange the third cake layer on top and repeat the process of adding the buttercream and compote again. Top with the final cake layer and cover the top and sides of the cake with the remaining buttercream. Refrigerate before serving and decorate the top of the cake with blackberries and blueberries when ready to serve. Store covered in the refrigerator for up to 4 days.

Black Currant Sweet Buns

Black currants are sweet and tart all at once and have a beautiful and glossy deep purple, almost black, exterior. They taste earthy and leave you with a lingering aromatic experience. Wrapping black currants inside a sweet dough helps preserve that experience for as long as possible, delivering a flavorsome sensation with each jammy bite. If you can't get your hands on fresh black currants, I suggest looking for black currant jam to substitute. Otherwise, you can use other berries, such as blueberries or blackberries, though you won't achieve the same sweet tang as from black currants.

Makes 12 buns

❖ **FOR THE BUN DOUGH**

1 cup (240 ml) milk

½ cup plus 1 tablespoon (125 g) lightly salted butter

5 cups (600 g) all-purpose flour

½ cup (100 g) granulated sugar

4 teaspoons (½ ounce / 14 g) instant yeast

1 teaspoon ground cinnamon

1 large egg, at room temperature

❖ **FOR THE FILLING**

8 ounces (225 g) black currants

2 tablespoons granulated sugar

8 oz (225 g) cream cheese

1 cup (120 g) confectioners' sugar

For the bun dough, in a small saucepan, warm the milk and butter over medium heat until the butter has melted.

In the bowl of a stand mixer fitted with the dough hook attachment, combine the flour, granulated sugar, yeast, and cinnamon. Add the milk mixture and the egg and knead on medium-low for 8 to 10 minutes, or until the dough is soft and elastic. Transfer the dough to a lightly buttered bowl, cover with a tea towel, and let rise in a warm spot for about 1 ½ hours, or until doubled in size.

For the filling, in a small saucepan, bring the black currants, granulated sugar, and 1 tablespoon of water to a simmer, then lower the heat and cook for about 5 minutes, or until the berries are soft but still intact and the compote has thickened. Set aside.

In a medium bowl, combine the cream cheese and confectioners' sugar. Set aside.

Preheat the oven to 425°F (220°C). Line 2 baking sheets with parchment paper.

Once the dough has doubled in size, place on a well-floured surface. Using a rolling pin and more flour as needed to prevent sticking, roll out the dough into a large rectangle, measuring roughly 22 x 18 inches (55 x 45 cm) with the long sides horizontal. Spread the cream cheese mixture over the entire surface of the dough, all the way to the edges. Spread the black currant compote in evenly spaced, thick vertical lines on top of the cream cheese mixture. Starting on 1 of the shorter sides, gently roll the dough from left to right to form a log. Using a sharp knife, cut the log into 12 even pieces. Arrange the buns on the prepared baking sheets and bake, 1 baking sheet at a time, for 10 to 12 minutes, or until nicely browned. Set on a wire rack to cool completely before serving. Store in an airtight bag at room temperature for up to 2 days.

No-Knead Wild Blueberry and Oregano Bread

Tossing *bilberries* — "wild blueberries" — on bread dough and then baking it so they burst and bleed into the bread is one of my favorite ways to highlight these berries. They offer a slightly sweet, jammy flavor that balances the pop of fresh oregano and sea salt. I love serving this bread warm with some good oil and homemade farmhouse cheese. If you don't have wild blueberries, you can use regular blueberries or blackberries. Plan to start this recipe a day in advance.

Makes 1 loaf

3 cups (360 g) strong white bread flour

1 teaspoon salt

1 teaspoon (⅛ ounce / 3.5 g) instant yeast

1¼ cups (300 ml) warm water

2 teaspoons mild-flavored oil

1 cup (125 g) wild blueberries

1 teaspoon sea salt, plus more for serving

1 tablespoon fresh oregano leaves, plus more for serving

In a large bowl, whisk together the flour, salt, and yeast. Stir in the warm water and combine to form a soft dough. Cover with plastic wrap and let rise in a warm spot overnight (8 to 12 hours), or until bubbly and doubled in size.

Once the dough has doubled in size, preheat the oven to 425°F (220°C). Line a baking sheet with parchment paper and sprinkle some flour on the parchment.

Turn the dough out onto the prepared baking sheet. With floured hands, fold the dough over itself a few times. Drizzle the oil on top and gently press the dough down with your hands to form a flat, round shape, roughly 8 ½ inches (22 cm) in diameter. Spread the blueberries evenly on top of the dough and use your hands to gently press them into the dough a little. Sprinkle the sea salt and oregano on top. Bake for about 40 minutes, or until golden brown. Let cool for 10 minutes, then garnish with a little more sea salt and oregano and serve warm. Store leftovers in an airtight bag at room temperature for 1 to 2 days.

Yeast Bread

Settekake is a simple yeast bread, similar to pita and cooked on top of a *takke* (a Norwegian griddle). Before the use of ovens, yeast breads were cooked on griddles or hot stones or in pots. This way of cooking meant the breads needed to be round, as well as thinner than bread baked in an oven, so they would cook quickly and develop a golden-brown exterior and a soft interior.

These breads are especially delicious straight off the griddle and warm. A slab of good butter melting into a yellow puddle on top and a couple slices of Norwegian brown cheese sticking to it makes for a very delicious moment. The versatility of this type of bread means you can serve it with a sweet topping, as a savory wrap, or alongside a good thick soup.

Makes 10 breads

1 cup (240 ml) milk

4 tablespoons (56 g) lightly salted butter

7 cups (840 g) strong white bread flour

4 teaspoons (½ ounce / 14 g) instant yeast

1 teaspoon salt

In a small saucepan, warm the milk, butter, and 1 cup (240 ml) of water over medium-low heat until the butter has melted and the liquid is just warm to the touch.

In the bowl of a stand mixer fitted with the dough hook attachment, combine the flour, yeast, and salt. Add the milk mixture and knead on medium for about 5 minutes, or until the dough is soft and pliable. Transfer the dough to a lightly buttered bowl, cover with a tea towel, and let rise in a warm spot for about 45 minutes, or until doubled in size.

Once the dough has doubled in size, place on a lightly floured surface and divide into 10 equal pieces. Using a rolling pin and more flour as needed to prevent sticking, roll out each piece of dough into a circular shape that is roughly 6 inches (15 cm) in diameter and ½ inch (1.25 cm) thick. Cover with a tea towel.

Heat a takke over medium heat or place a large frying pan directly on the stove over medium heat. Put the fan on and open a window if possible. Place a couple of the dough rounds on the dry, hot takke (or 1 to 2 dough rounds if using a pan) and cook for about 5 minutes, or until golden and cooked through. Flip the breads and cook for about 5 minutes more, or until the other side is golden. Repeat to cook the remaining breads.

Serve warm with melted butter and brown cheese or alongside soups and stews. Store leftovers in an airtight container at room temperature for up to 3 days.

Trondheim's Wreath with Almonds and Raisins

This sweet wreath hails from Trondheim, the third largest city in the country and once the Viking capital of Norway. The name combines the words *trønder*, which refers to a person from the counties of Trønderlag, and rose, the symbol of the city since at least the sixteenth century. The shape is meant to convey the official flower, the four-petal dog rose. What makes *trønderrose* unique from other sweet breads is the lemon zest. It's bright and refreshing, much like the city itself.

Serves 10

❖ **FOR THE DOUGH**

4 cups (480 g) all-purpose flour

½ cup (100 g) granulated sugar

2 teaspoons (¼ ounce / 7 g) instant yeast

¼ teaspoon salt

2 teaspoons fresh lemon zest

1 cup (240 ml) lukewarm milk

½ cup (112 g) lightly salted butter, melted

1 large egg, at room temperature

❖ **FOR THE FILLING**

4 tablespoons (56 g) lightly salted butter, at room temperature

¼ cup (50 g) granulated sugar

1 teaspoon ground cinnamon

¾ cup (120 g) raisins

½ cup (60 g) almonds, chopped

❖ **FOR THE TOPPING**

1 large egg, at room temperature

Pearl sugar

Sliced almonds

For the dough, in a stand mixer fitted with the paddle attachment, combine the flour, granulated sugar, yeast, salt, lemon zest, lukewarm milk, melted butter, and the egg. Knead on medium for about 5 minutes, or until the dough is soft and elastic. Transfer the dough to a lightly buttered bowl, cover with a tea towel, and let rise in a warm spot for about 1 hour, or until doubled in size.

For the filling, in a medium bowl, beat together the butter, granulated sugar, and cinnamon. Set aside.

Once the dough has doubled in size, preheat the oven to 400°F (200°C). Line a baking sheet with parchment paper.

Place the dough on a lightly floured surface. Using a rolling pin and more flour as needed to prevent sticking, roll out the dough into a rectangle that measures roughly 30 x 10 inch (75 x 25 cm) with the long sides horizontal. Using a spatula, spread the butter mixture evenly across the dough, all the way to the edges, then sprinkle the raisins and chopped almonds on top. Starting on 1 of the long sides, roll the dough around the filling to form a log. Using a sharp knife, divide the log lengthwise in half. Place the two halves next to each other, cut side facing up, and braid them by alternating each dough half over the other, keeping the open layers on top. Pinch the ends together to seal. Take one end of the braid and roll it tightly inwards to create a circle or wreath. Place the wreath on the prepared baking sheet, cover with a tea towel, and let rise in a warm spot for 30 minutes.

For the topping, in a small bowl, whisk the egg. Using a pastry brush, lightly brush the egg on the dough. Generously sprinkle the top with pearl sugar and sliced almonds. Bake for 25 to 30 minutes, or until golden brown. Transfer to a wire rack to cool slightly before serving. Store in an airtight bag at room temperature for up to 2 days.

Lemon Golden Cake with Clovers

Gullkake means "golden cake" and typically refers to the abundance of egg yolks used in the batter to give this cake its lovely glow. In the summer, I like to add in lemon to brighten up the flavor, and sprinkle red clover petals on top for a beautiful finish and naturally sweet taste. Clovers grow all around us, giving us a plentiful supply but feel free to use other edible flower petals local to you for that floral touch.

Serves 12

❖ **FOR THE CAKE**

3 cups (360 g) all-purpose flour

1 teaspoon baking powder

1 teaspoon baking soda

½ teaspoon salt

4 large egg yolks, plus 2 large eggs, at room temperature

1½ cups (300 g) granulated sugar

¾ cup (170 g) lightly salted butter, at room temperature

¾ cup (180 ml) sour cream

Zest and juice of 1 lemon

❖ **FOR THE GLAZE**

1 large egg white, at room temperature

1½ teaspoons freshly squeezed lemon juice

1¼ cups (150 g) confectioners' sugar

❖ **FOR SERVING**

Red clover petals

For the cake, preheat the oven to 350°F (180°C). Butter and flour a 10 to 12 cup Bundt pan.

In a medium bowl, whisk together the flour, baking powder, baking soda, and salt.

In a stand mixer fitted with the whisk attachment, combine the 4 egg yolks (not the whole eggs) with ½ cup (100 g) of the granulated sugar and whip on medium-high for about 5 minutes, or until light and fluffy. Pour the egg mixture into a medium bowl.

Wipe the stand mixer clean and fit it with the paddle attachment. Add the butter and the remaining 1 cup (200 g) of granulated sugar and beat on medium-high for about 1 minute, or until light and fluffy. Add the 2 whole eggs and beat to incorporate. Add the egg yolk and sugar mixture, along with the sour cream, lemon zest, and lemon juice and beat to combine. Add the flour mixture and beat until well combined. Scrape the batter into the prepared pan and smooth the top. Bake for about 50 minutes, or until a toothpick inserted in the center comes out clean and the top of the cake is golden brown. Let the cake cool in the pan for 8 to 10 minutes and not longer. Carefully invert the cake onto a wire rack and let cool completely.

For the glaze, in a medium bowl, lightly whisk the egg white and lemon juice. Gradually whisk in the confectioners' sugar, adding more or less as needed, until smooth and combined. Drizzle the glaze on top of the cooled cake, then sprinkle clover petals over the glaze. Store in an airtight container at room temperature for up to 5 days.

Fireweed Collar Cookies

Rows of purple-pink fireweed (also known as rosebay willowherb and great willowherb) line the landscape at this time of year. Their shoots emerge in spring and by late summer they blossom. By autumn, they become tall, woolly-looking stalks of seeds with silky hairs to be spread by the wind before winter arrives.

Fireweed is one of those incredible wild plants that is both beautiful and edible. After a forest fire, it's one of the first plants to return, making it an important part of managing land and encouraging regrowth, and also how it earned its name.

I like to add the petals into traditional *snipp*, fluffy cookies shaped in the form of a collar or diamond. While the sweet petals don't infuse much flavor, they provide a good source of nutrients and make for the most beautiful cookies. You can easily replace the petals with other edible flowers.

Makes about 30 cookies

3½ cups (420 g) all-purpose flour

1 cup (200 g) granulated sugar, plus more for finishing

1½ teaspoons baking soda

½ teaspoon ground cardamom

½ cup (112 g) lightly salted butter, melted and cooled

1 cup (240 ml) buttermilk

1 large handful fireweed petals

Preheat the oven to 400°F (200°C). Line a baking sheet with parchment paper.

In a large bowl, whisk together the flour, sugar, baking soda, and cardamom.

In a small bowl, combine the cooled melted butter and the buttermilk. Add to the flour mixture and combine to form a soft dough. Gently fold in the fireweed petals.

On a well-floured surface, using a rolling pin and more flour as needed to prevent sticking, roll out the dough until about ½ inch (1.25 cm) thick. Using a small knife, cut out about 30 "collar" or diamond shapes, each about 4 inches (10 cm) long. Arrange some of the cookies on the prepared baking sheet, leaving space in between, and sprinkle the tops with sugar. Bake for 10 to 12 minutes, or until golden. Transfer to a wire rack to cool. Repeat to bake the remaining cookies. Store in an airtight container at room temperature for up to 1 week.

Cloudberry Custard Meringue Cake

Multer i himmelseng translates to "cloudberries in a heavenly bed," and heavenly is the perfect description for this cake layered with custard, meringue, and fresh cloudberries. It's a summer treasure since cloudberries, referred to as the mountain's gold, grow briefly and sparingly. Feel free to experiment with other berries, such as yellow raspberries or even fruit like peaches, if cloudberries are difficult to find.

Serves 10

❖ **FOR THE CAKE**

3 large eggs, at room temperature

½ cup (100 g) granulated sugar

1 cup (120 g) all-purpose flour

½ teaspoon baking powder

❖ **FOR THE CUSTARD**

2 tablespoons granulated sugar

3 large egg yolks, at room temperature

1½ teaspoons cornstarch

¾ cup plus 1 tablespoon (200 ml) crème fraîche

1 teaspoon vanilla extract

❖ **FOR THE MERINGUE**

3 large egg whites, at room temperature

¾ cup (150 g) granulated sugar

❖ **FOR FINISHING**

1¼ cups (125 g) cloudberries

For the cake, preheat the oven to 325°F (165°C). Cut a round piece of parchment paper so it fits perfectly in the bottom of a 9 inch (23 cm) springform pan. Butter the pan, then add the parchment and butter it.

In a stand mixer fitted with the whisk attachment, whip the eggs and sugar on medium-high for about 5 minutes, or until light and fluffy. Sift the flour and baking powder over the batter and use a spatula to gently fold until combined. Pour into the prepared pan and set on a baking sheet. Bake for 20 to 25 minutes, or until golden brown. Let cool completely in the pan. Raise the oven temperature to 400°F (200°C).

For the custard, in a large bowl, whisk together the sugar and egg yolks. Add the cornstarch and whisk until thick and pale yellow.

In a small saucepan, warm the crème fraîche and vanilla over low heat until just beginning to simmer then remove from the heat. Slowly add the crème fraîche mixture to the egg yolk mixture, whisking constantly to avoid curdling the eggs. Pour the mixture back into the saucepan and place over medium heat. Cook, stirring constantly, until thick. Set aside to cool.

For the meringue, in a stand mixer fitted with the whisk attachment, whip the egg whites on medium until foamy. Gradually add the sugar, whipping until stiff glossy peaks form.

Pour the custard over the cake in the pan, spreading it just to the edges of the cake. Place the cloudberries on top of the custard. Using a spatula, gently spread the meringue on top of the cloudberries, using sweeping motions to create waves. Bake for about 15 minutes, or until golden on top. Let cool completely in the pan before serving. Keep covered in the refrigerator for up to 3 days.

Buttery Caraway and Jarlsberg Crackers

Along the dry meadow slopes, you'll find native caraway growing throughout the country, with its feathery green leaves swaying in summer's gentle breeze. Caraway seeds have a mild anise flavor that most will associate with sauerkraut. It's long been used for helping with digestion, as well as flavoring spirits, breads, meat dishes, and cheeses like traditional *pultost*.

While caraway grows wild here, cultivation is centered in the municipality of Inderøy in Trøndelag. It was there, a few summers ago, along Den Gyldne Omvei, "the Golden Road," that I discovered just how many culinary uses there are for the seeds. Caraway crackers were being sold in the boutiques and I knew I had to make my own when I returned home. I keep it simple and add some Jarlsberg cheese, which has complimentary nutty notes. These crackers have a sharpness, but it's mellowed by their buttery richness. Share these on a table filled with fresh salads, summer fruits, cured meats, and vegetables. They're meant to be savored.

Makes about 18 crackers

1 cup (120 g) all-purpose flour

½ cup (112 g) lightly salted butter, at room temperature

1¼ cups (120 g) grated Jarlsberg cheese

1 tablespoon dried caraway seeds

¼ teaspoon salt

In a large bowl, combine the flour, butter, cheese, caraway seeds, and salt and use your hands to form a soft dough. Cover and refrigerate for 1 hour.

Preheat the oven to 400°F (200°C). Line a baking sheet with parchment paper.

On a lightly floured surface, using a rolling pin and more flour as needed, roll out the dough until about ¼ inch (about 6 mm) thick. Using a 2¾ inches (7 cm) round cookie cutter or the rim of a large glass, cut out circles in the dough. Place the crackers on the prepared baking sheet and bake for 10 to 12 minutes, or until golden. Transfer to a wire rack to cool. Store at room temperature in an airtight container for up to 2 weeks.

Mini Potato Flatbreads with Roasted Tomatoes and Caramelized Onions

One of my favorite little dishes to serve when the summer tomatoes are ripe and plentiful and the onions are sweet are these *lomper* with roasted tomatoes and caramelized onions. They're just summer bliss, and each little bite is full of flavor. By frying the lomper, their taste becomes more prominent, and they have a slight sweetness, making them an ideal base for these toppings.

Makes about 24 flatbreads

17½ ounces (500 g) cherry tomatoes, cut in half

5 tablespoons mild-flavored oil, plus more for frying

Sea salt and black pepper

1¾ pounds (800 g) onions, thinly sliced

2 teaspoons fresh thyme leaves

6 to 8 Soft Spelt Potato Flatbreads (*Speltlomper*; page 73)

Preheat the oven to 400°F (200°C).

Spread the tomatoes, cut-side up, on a rimmed baking sheet. Toss with 2 tablespoons of the oil and sprinkle with salt and pepper. Roast for about 25 minutes, or until soft and fragrant. Set aside and cover to keep warm.

In a large pan, heat the remaining 3 tablespoons of oil over medium-high heat. Add the onions and thyme and season with salt and pepper. Lower the heat to medium-low and cook, stirring occasionally, for 20 to 25 minutes, or until the onions are soft and golden brown. Transfer the onions to a separate dish and cover to keep warm.

Using a round cookie cutter, cut 3 to 4 small circles from each lomper. Cut the leftover lomper scraps into small, thin pieces.

Line a large plate with paper towels.

Place the pan used to cook the onions over medium-high heat and add enough oil to thinly and evenly coat the bottom. Working in batches, add a few lomper rounds to the pan and cook for 30 to 45 seconds, or until golden brown on the bottom. Flip the lomper and cook for 30 to 45 seconds, or until the other side is golden brown. Transfer to the paper towel-lined plate. Add a little more oil to the pan then toss in the lomper scraps and cook, stirring often, for about 3 minutes, or until golden brown all over. Transfer to the paper towel-lined plate.

Place the lomper rounds on a serving platter and top with the caramelized onions followed by the roasted tomatoes and the fried lomper scraps to finish. Serve immediately.

Fire
& Ice

❖   Ild og is

❖ **THE LONG SUMMER DAYS FADE GENTLY** into autumn's cloak of rich colors. Autumn has its subtle and quiet moments, from the falling leaves to the way the breeze whispers along still paths. It also has moments of fierceness, such as when the sky opens up in a blaze of brilliant orange and red, and when we say goodnight to a warm day only to find frost's breath covering the land in the morning. It has the momentum of two opposing forces, like fire and ice, with each element bringing a strength to the season that enlivens it even more. The day can start with a bright blue sky and finish with a dramatic and fiery sunset.

The harvest season reaches its culmination, with an array of ingredients, all bursting with flavor and color. Apples, pears, root vegetables, and wild edibles scattered along the forest floor are some of the highlights. It's a lavish season, when *koselig*, "coziness," is worn like a sweater. Warm spices, outdoor fires, hikes into the woods, and friendly gatherings add joy to the moments. Bright baked goods like apple cakes, tea bread, and lingonberry hand pies turn into hearty chocolate desserts, caramel-drenched roll cakes, and traditional breads to serve with rich stews. The kitchen celebrates the growing season as we begin to prepare for the onset of winter.

Apple Cake with Salted Gin Caramel

A quick drive through our valley in autumn will draw your eyes to craggy apple trees dotted with bright reds and pinks and subtle greens. As the season moves forward, the ground below is strewn with fallen fruit, inviting you to make countless dishes. One of my favorite treats to prepare, as soon as the first of the apples are ripe, is apple cake. I often serve it with whipped cream, but for a little indulgence, I drizzle salted gin caramel on top, because apples and caramel are best friends and when they invite gin along it becomes a party.

Serves 8 to 10

❖ FOR THE CAKE

1¾ cups (210 g) all-purpose flour

1½ teaspoons baking powder

⅔ cup (150 g) lightly salted butter,
   at room temperature

1 cup (200 g) granulated sugar

3 large eggs, at room temperature

½ cup (120 ml) milk

3 to 4 tart apples, peeled, cored,
   and thinly sliced

Cinnamon and pearl sugar,
   for decorating

❖ FOR THE GIN CARAMEL

1 cup (200 g) granulated sugar

6 tablespoons (84 g) lightly
   salted butter

½ cup (120 ml) heavy cream

2 tablespoons Norwegian gin

1 teaspoon flaky sea salt

For the cake, preheat the oven to 350°F (180°C). Butter an 8 inch (20 cm) springform pan.

In a medium bowl, whisk together the flour and baking powder.

In the bowl of a stand mixer fitted with the paddle attachment, combine the butter and granulated sugar and beat until light and fluffy. Add the eggs, 1 at a time, incorporating each egg before adding the next, and beat for 2 to 3 minutes, or until light and creamy. Add the flour mixture and beat to incorporate. Slowly add the milk and beat just until well blended. Pour half of the batter into the prepared pan. Spread half of the apple slices on top, pressing them into the batter, then sprinkle with a little cinnamon. Pour the remaining batter on top of the apples, then arrange the remaining apples, in concentric circles, on top. Sprinkle with cinnamon and pearl sugar. Bake for about 40 minutes, or until a toothpick inserted in the center comes out clean and the cake is golden brown. Cool slightly in the pan.

For the gin caramel, in a medium saucepan, heat the granulated sugar over medium heat, stirring constantly with a wooden spoon, for 5 to 8 minutes, or until it turns a deep amber color. Add the butter, being careful, as it will bubble up fiercely, and stir until melted. Carefully stir in the heavy cream and let the mixture boil for 1 minute. Add the gin and flaky sea salt and stir until smooth. Remove from the heat and let cool for 10 minutes. Transfer to a clean glass jar and let cool at room temperature.

Serve the warm cake with the caramel sauce alongside. Keep the cake in an airtight container at room temperature for up to 2 days or in the refrigerator for about 4 days. Leftover caramel can be stored in an airtight container in the refrigerator for up to 1 month.

Potato Tarts with Spiced Stewed Apples

Potetterte is a traditional type of puff pastry made with equal parts potatoes, flour, and butter. In a cookbook from the 1950s, I saw it described as the cheapest and simplest way to make a version of *bløtkake*, a layered cream cake, with the pastry replacing the sponge cake layers. It was commonly made during war times when rations were in place, and often served with coffee made from dried yellow peas browned in the oven.

Despite being a cheaper alternative, these tarts are flavorsome, flaky, and buttery. Some recipes call for one large tart, while others call for individual tarts. I like the idea of each person having their own. Applesauce is the typical filling, but I've added in a bit of spice and kept the apples somewhat intact for texture.

Serves 5

5½ ounces (150 g) starchy potatoes

1¼ cups (150 g) all-purpose flour

⅔ cup (150 g) lightly salted butter, at room temperature

8 small, firm and tart apples, diced with skins on (about 5 cups)

½ cup (100 g) granulated sugar

1 teaspoon ground cardamom

½ teaspoon ground cinnamon

¼ teaspoon ground cloves

⅛ teaspoon salt

1 tablespoon freshly squeezed lemon juice

Whipped cream and confectioners' sugar, for serving

In a medium pot, cover the potatoes with cold water and bring to a boil. Lower the heat and simmer for 10 to 15 minutes, or until the potatoes are tender when pierced with a knife. Drain the potatoes and let cool.

Once the potatoes are cool, peel and run through a ricer into a large bowl, or mash by hand until completely smooth. Add the flour and butter and mix to form a smooth dough. Cover and refrigerate.

In a medium saucepan, bring the apples, granulated sugar, cardamom, cinnamon, cloves, salt, lemon juice, and ⅓ cup (80 ml) of water to a simmer over medium heat. Continue simmering for about 5 minutes, or until the apples have softened. Using a fork, roughly mash the apples, leaving chunkier pieces, then set aside to cool.

Preheat the oven to 400°F (200°C). Line a baking sheet with parchment paper.

Place the dough on a lightly floured surface. Using a rolling pin and more flour as needed to prevent sticking, roll out the dough until about ½ inch (1.25 cm) thick. Using a 3 inch (7.5 cm) round cookie cutter or the rim of a glass, cut out 15 small circles. Place the circles of dough on the prepared baking sheet. Using a fork, poke holes in the dough. Bake for 25 to 30 minutes, or until golden brown. Transfer to a wire rack and let cool.

To assemble, place 5 pastry circles on a serving platter. Divide half of the applesauce among the pastry circles, then top each with a second pastry circle. Divide the remaining applesauce among the second layer of pastry circles and finish with the remaining pastry circles. Top each tart with some whipped cream and dust with confectioners' sugar before serving.

Plum and Sour Cream Cake

As autumn carries on, there's always a burst of excitement when we look down by the old barn and all of a sudden see our plum tree full of bright and deep purple plums. They seem to ripen overnight. The tree that was once bare has branches hanging heavy with what looks like a never-ending supply of luscious plums.

For a special treat, I like to make this simple cake of plums blanketed in batter made with sour cream. It's incredibly moist and delicate, offering a good balance of tartness and sweetness. If you find your plums are really tart, you may wish to sprinkle a little bit of sugar on top before pouring the batter over them. Serve this cake warm with some whipped cream or vanilla ice cream.

Serves 8

12 ounces (350 g) plums, cored and halved

1½ cups (180 g) all-purpose flour

1½ teaspoons baking powder

¼ teaspoon salt

½ cup (112 g) lightly salted butter, at room temperature

¾ cup plus 2 tablespoons (175 g) granulated sugar, plus more for sprinkling

2 large eggs, at room temperature

1 teaspoon vanilla extract

½ cup (120 ml) sour cream

2 tablespoons sliced almonds

Whipped cream or vanilla ice cream, for serving

Preheat the oven to 350°F (180°C).

Cut a round piece of parchment paper so it fits perfectly in the bottom of a 9 inch (23 cm) springform pan. Butter the pan, then add the parchment and butter it.

Arrange the plums, cut-side up, evenly across the bottom of the prepared pan.

In a medium bowl, whisk together the flour, baking powder and salt.

In the bowl a stand mixer fitted with the paddle attachment, beat the butter and sugar until light and fluffy. Add the eggs, 1 at a time, incorporating each egg before adding the next, and beat for 2 to 3 minutes, or until light and creamy. Add the vanilla and sour cream and beat until fully combined. Add the flour mixture and beat until just combined. Using a spatula, carefully spread the batter over the plums in the pan and smooth the top. Scatter the sliced almonds and sprinkle about ¼ cup (50 g) of sugar on top of the batter. Bake for 35 to 40 minutes, or until a toothpick inserted in the center comes out clean and the top of the cake is golden brown. Cool slightly in the pan before serving with whipped cream or vanilla ice cream. Keep covered in the refrigerator for up to 3 days.

Lingonberry and Cream Layer Cake

One of my favorite cakes, *bløtkake*, gets a little makeover with lingonberries. The cream and the sponge are nicely balanced with the lingonberry sauce, while the sugared berries offer a unique texture that pairs nicely with the softness of the cake. There's a little tartness when you first bite into it, but then the flavors blend into a symphony of sensations. You can substitute the lingonberries with cranberries.

Serves 8 to 10

❖ **FOR THE CAKE**

5 large eggs, at room temperature

¾ cup plus 2 tablespoons (175 g) granulated sugar

1½ cups (180 g) all-purpose flour

1 teaspoon baking powder

❖ **FOR THE SAUCE**

5¼ ounces (150 g) fresh or frozen lingonberries

1½ cups (300 g) granulated sugar

❖ **FOR THE SUGARED LINGONBERRIES**

½ cup (100 g) granulated sugar, plus more for rolling

7 ounces (200 g) fresh or frozen lingonberries

❖ **FOR THE WHIPPED CREAM**

3 cups (720 ml) heavy cream

2½ tablespoons confectioners' sugar

For the cake, preheat the oven to 325°F (165°C).

Cut a round piece of parchment paper so it fits perfectly in the bottom of a 9 inch (23 cm) springform pan. Butter the pan, then add the parchment and butter it.

In a stand mixer fitted with the whisk attachment, whip the eggs and granulated sugar on medium-high for 6 to 8 minutes, or until stiff and light in color. Sift the flour and baking powder over the batter and use a spatula to gently fold until just combined. Pour into the prepared pan and set on a baking sheet. Bake for 35 to 40 minutes, or until golden brown. Let cool completely.

For the sauce, in a small saucepan, combine the lingonberries, granulated sugar, and a spoonful of water and cook over low heat, stirring occasionally, for 10 to 15 minutes, or until the berries soften and burst. Set aside to cool.

For the sugared berries, in a medium saucepan, bring the granulated sugar and 2 cups (480 ml) of water to a simmer over medium heat, stirring until the sugar dissolves. Lower the heat, add the lingonberries, and leave undisturbed for 2 minutes. If using frozen berries, let them sit in the pan a little longer. Using a slotted spoon, transfer the berries to a wire rack or a perforated baking sheet, spread them in a single layer, and let dry for about 25 minutes.

After about 25 minutes, place some granulated sugar in a bowl and roll the berries in the sugar to coat.

For the whipped cream, whip the heavy cream and confectioners' sugar until stiff peaks form.

To assemble, cut the cake horizontally into 3 even layers. Spoon half of the lingonberry sauce over the bottom layer then top with a generous amount of whipped cream, spreading it to the edges of the cake. Arrange the second layer of cake on top and add the rest of the lingonberry sauce and more whipped cream, reserving enough whipped cream to cover the cake. Arrange the final cake layer on top then cover the top and sides of the cake with the remaining whipped cream and place the sugared berries on top. The cake can be served immediately or made up to 1 day in advance, which allows the cake to soften and soak up more flavor. Keep covered in the refrigerator for up to 3 days.

Troll Cream Brown Sugar Oatmeal Cookie Sandwiches

Trollkrem, or "troll cream," is a traditional dessert made with lingonberries, whipped egg whites, and sugar. The name possibly derives from the term *trollbœr*, which translates to "troll berry" and in earlier times referred to inedible and tart berries. Nowadays, it feels more natural to attribute the enchanting name to the dessert's airy texture and, perhaps, to the trolls living in the forest with lingonberries adorning their feet.

These cookie sandwiches are a play on this dessert and the rocky terrain where the trolls are said to dwell. The troll cream, made up of cream cheese rather than egg whites, is sandwiched between soft and knobbly oatmeal cookies with a hint of cardamom. If lingonberries are hard to come by, substitute with chopped cranberries. Enjoy these charming cookies knowing that wild lingonberries (and maybe trolls) are popping up along the forest bed.

Makes 9 cookies

❖ **FOR THE COOKIES**

½ cup plus 2 tablespoons (100 g) dark brown sugar

2 tablespoons granulated sugar

½ cup (112 g) lightly salted butter, melted

1 large egg, at room temperature

½ teaspoon vanilla extract

1 cup (120 g) all-purpose flour

½ cup (50 g) quick-cooking oats

½ teaspoon ground cardamom

½ teaspoon salt

½ teaspoon baking powder

¼ teaspoon baking soda

❖ **FOR THE TROLL CREAM**

½ cup (50 g) lingonberries

¼ cup (50 g) granulated sugar

¼ cup (56 g) cream cheese

4 tablespoons (56 g) lightly salted butter, at room temperature

1 cup (120 g) confectioners' sugar

For the cookies, in a medium bowl, whisk together the brown sugar, granulated sugar, and melted butter. Whisk in the egg and vanilla until combined.

In a large bowl, whisk together the flour, oats, cardamom, salt, baking powder, and baking soda. Add the flour mixture to the egg mixture and stir until well blended. Cover and refrigerate for at least 1 hour.

For the troll cream, in a small saucepan, combine the lingonberries and granulated sugar and cook over medium heat for about 10 minutes, or until the sugar dissolves and the jam thickens. Set aside to cool completely.

Preheat the oven to 350°F (180°C). Line 2 baking sheets with parchment paper.

Scoop the cookie dough into 18 equal balls and divide among the baking sheets. Bake, 1 baking sheet at a time, for 10 to 12 minutes, or until golden brown. Transfer to a wire rack to cool.

Once the lingonberry jam is cool, in a large bowl, beat the cream cheese and butter until light and fluffy. Add the confectioners' sugar, then add the cooled lingonberry jam and fold until combined.

To assemble, spread a good amount of troll cream on the bottoms of half of the cookies. Place the remaining cookies on top of the troll cream to form sandwiches. Store in the refrigerator until ready to serve or for up to 3 days.

Rustic Apple, Lingonberry, and Cardamom Hand Pies

These little hand pies combine autumn's apples and lingonberries into irresistible cardamom-spiced pastry pockets that are full of flavor and easy to serve. They're quite fun to assemble, as you make them from scratch, and any imperfections in shape and size will only add to their homemade charm. You might end up with some juice that runs out during baking, but just scoop it up and drizzle it over the pies when you're ready to serve. A good dollop of whipped cream or vanilla ice cream would be heavenly with these.

Makes 8 hand pies

❖ **FOR THE CRUST**

2 ¼ cups (270 g) all-purpose flour

1 tablespoon granulated sugar

½ tablespoon ground cardamom

½ teaspoon salt

1 cup (224 g) lightly salted butter, cut into cubes and chilled

½ cup (120 ml) sour cream

❖ **FOR THE FILLING**

1 medium sweet and tart apple, cored and diced

4 ½ ounces (125 g) fresh or frozen lingonberries (or chopped cranberries)

⅓ cup (65 g) granulated sugar

½ tablespoon all-purpose flour

¼ teaspoon ground cinnamon

❖ **FOR FINISHING**

1 large egg, at room temperature

Pearl sugar

For the crust, in a large bowl, whisk together the flour, granulated sugar, cardamom, and salt. Using a pastry cutter or your hands, cut in the butter until the mixture resembles breadcrumbs. Add the sour cream and blend together with a fork. Gather the pastry dough together into a large ball, divide in half, and flatten each half into a disk. Wrap in plastic wrap and refrigerate for at least 1 hour.

Preheat the oven to 400°F (200°C). Line a baking sheet with parchment paper.

For the filling, in a large bowl, combine the apple, lingonberries, granulated sugar, flour, and cinnamon. Set aside.

Take the dough from the refrigerator, place on a lightly floured surface, and let stand for a few minutes at room temperature. Using a rolling pin and more flour as needed to prevent sticking, roll out each disk into a rectangle that measures 16 x 12 ½ inches (40 x 32 cm). Trim the edges to make them straight and reserve any extra dough. Cut 1 of the rectangles into 8 equal sections that measure 6 ¼ x 4 inches (16 x 10 cm). Repeat with the other rectangle. Place 8 of the sections on the prepared baking sheet. Divide the filling equally among the sections, spreading it in the middle and leaving space around the edges. Place the remaining dough sections on top. With a fork, crimp the edges of each pie to seal them closed. If you have trouble closing them, remove some of the filling. Use any extra dough to fill any gaps.

In a small bowl, whisk the egg with 1 teaspoon water. Using a pastry brush, lightly brush the egg wash on top of the pies and sprinkle with pearl sugar. Make a small cut on the top of each pie to release steam during baking. Bake for about 25 minutes, or until golden brown. Let cool before serving. Store covered in the refrigerator for up to 5 days.

Rye and Almond Honey Cake

The scent of sweet honey and nutty almond notes filling the room as this cake bakes is pure bliss. It's hearty with a hint of orange and ginger, and full of texture and crumb that will be enjoyed until the last bite. I prefer using a floral honey, as the more flavorful the honey is, the more fragrant this cake will be. If the honey is thick, I melt it over low heat until it's runny enough to use.

Serves 8 to 10

❖ **FOR THE CAKE**

⅔ cup (150 g) lightly salted butter, at room temperature

½ cup (100 g) granulated sugar

4 large eggs, at room temperature

¾ cup (180 ml) runny honey

Zest of 1 orange

1½ teaspoons grated fresh ginger

1¼ cups (150 g) light rye flour

1¼ cups (150 g) all-purpose flour

2 teaspoons baking powder

1½ teaspoons ground cinnamon

⅔ cup (110 g) ground almonds

❖ **FOR THE SYRUP**

Juice of ½ orange

3 tablespoons runny honey

For the cake, preheat the oven to 340°F (170°C). Butter an 8 inch (20 cm) springform pan.

In the bowl of a stand mixer fitted with the paddle attachment, combine the butter and sugar and beat until light and fluffy. Add the eggs, 1 at a time, incorporating each egg before adding the next, and beat for 2 to 3 minutes, or until light and creamy. Add the honey, orange zest, and ginger and beat until light and fluffy.

In a large bowl, whisk together the rye flour, all-purpose flour, baking powder, and cinnamon. Using a spatula, gently fold into the wet ingredients until just combined, then stir in the ground almonds. Pour the batter into the prepared pan and bake for 40 to 50 minutes, or until a toothpick inserted in the center comes out clean and the top of the cake is golden brown.

For the syrup, in a small bowl, whisk together the orange juice and honey. Brush it on top of the warm cake while it's cooling in the pan. Let the cake cool, then transfer to a plate and serve. Store at room temperature in an airtight container for up to 5 days.

Wild Mushroom Pancake Bake

I always return to these savory wild mushroom pancakes. They're creamy, earthy, meaty, and buttery all at once. While they're not the traditional way of serving Norwegian pancakes, they're everything I dream of when foraging in our mountains. If I'm low on wild mushrooms, I supplement with cremini mushrooms, so feel free to do the same here. These pancakes are slightly thicker than typical ones, so they can hold up to all the cheesy mushroom goodness.

Serves 8

❖ **FOR THE PANCAKES**

1½ cups (180 g) all-purpose flour

½ teaspoon salt

2 cups (480 ml) milk

4 large eggs, at room temperature

Butter, for cooking

❖ **FOR THE WHITE SAUCE**

4 tablespoons (56 g) lightly salted butter

½ cup (60 g) all-purpose flour

3 cups (720 ml) milk

½ teaspoon salt

¼ teaspoon ground nutmeg

❖ **FOR THE MUSHROOMS**

3 tablespoons lightly salted butter

17½ ounces (500 g) wild mushrooms, sliced

3 garlic cloves, sliced

1 tablespoon fresh thyme leaves

½ teaspoon salt

❖ **FOR ASSEMBLING**

5½ ounces (150 g) mixed Gouda and sharp white cheddar, grated

Sea salt, freshly ground black pepper, and fresh thyme sprigs

For the pancakes, in a large bowl, whisk together the flour and salt. Whisk in the milk, a little at a time, until you have a smooth batter without any lumps. Add the eggs and whisk to combine. Let stand for 15 to 20 minutes.

Heat a large frying pan over medium heat. Add enough butter to evenly coat the bottom when melted. When the butter is foaming, ladle in ¾ cup (180 ml) of the batter, moving the pan around to evenly coat the bottom. Cook for about 1 minute, or until the bottom of the pancake has set and turned golden. Flip the pancake and cook for about 1 minute more, or until the other side is golden brown. Transfer the pancake to a plate. Add more butter to the pan and repeat to make 5 more pancakes. Set aside.

For the white sauce, in a large saucepan, melt the butter over medium-high heat. Whisk in the flour and cook, whisking frequently, for about 2 minutes. Add the milk, salt, and nutmeg and cook, whisking frequently, until thick. Set aside.

For the mushrooms, in a large skillet, melt the butter over medium-high heat. Add the mushrooms, garlic, thyme, and salt and cook for about 10 minutes, or until the mushrooms are softened.

Preheat the oven to 425°F (220°C). Butter a large baking dish.

Arrange 2 pancakes on the bottom of the prepared baking dish, filling in any gaps by tearing off pieces from another pancake. Spread half of the white sauce on top of the pancakes then layer half of the cheese on top, followed by half of the mushrooms. Arrange 2 more pancakes on top, filling in any gaps with another pancake. Repeat the process of layering the remaining white sauce, cheese, and mushroom filling. Sprinkle with the sea salt, black pepper, and fresh thyme sprigs. Bake for 10 to 15 minutes, or until bubbling and golden. Let cool slightly before serving.

Soft Root Vegetable Flatbreads

Using root vegetables to make traditional *lomper* is a marvelous way to pack in more nutrients while also adding unique flavor. Sweet potatoes and carrots impart sweetness, while red beets and parsnips lean into earthy notes. I like to add spices for a stronger flavor, but you can leave them out. These *lomper* are all made using the same basic procedure, but the root vegetables cook for different times and are combined with slightly different ingredient combinations—follow the recipe for the specifics.

Makes 10 lomper for each root vegetable (40 lomper total)

❖ FOR THE CARROT FLATBREADS

5 large carrots, peeled and cut into chunks

¾ cup (90 g) light rye flour

¾ cup (90 g) all-purpose flour

¾ teaspoon salt

¼ teaspoon dried dill (optional)

¼ teaspoon cumin seeds (optional)

❖ FOR THE SWEET POTATO FLATBREADS

1 pound (450 g) sweet potatoes, peeled and cut into chunks

⅓ cup (40 g) light rye flour

½ cup (60 g) all-purpose flour

¾ teaspoon salt

¼ teaspoon toasted cardamom seeds (optional)

¼ teaspoon coriander seeds (optional)

❖ FOR THE PARSNIP FLATBREADS

14½ ounces (415 g) parsnips, peeled and cut into chunks

1 cup (120 g) all-purpose flour

¾ teaspoon salt

¼ teaspoon fennel seeds (optional)

¼ teaspoon sesame seeds (optional)

Cook each root vegetable separately: In a large pot, cover the carrots, sweet potatoes, parsnips, or red beets with cold water and bring to a boil. Lower the heat and simmer until the vegetables are tender when pierced with a knife—8 to 10 minutes for the carrots, 15 to 20 minutes for the potatoes or parsnips, and about 30 minutes for the red beets. Drain and cool slightly.

Purée each root vegetable separately: Purée the carrots in a blender then transfer to a large bowl.

Run the sweet potatoes or parsnips through a ricer into a large bowl or mash by hand until completely smooth.

Let the beets cool completely, then peel off the skins and remove the stems. Purée in a blender until smooth, then transfer to a large bowl.

Make each kind of lompe separately: Add the flours, salt, and spices, if using, to each kind of puréed vegetable and mix until the dough is soft and pliable but not dry. If the dough is very wet, gradually add a small amount of flour and mix until the dough is soft and pliable.

Shape the lomper: Working with one kind of dough as a time, divide the dough into 10 equal pieces, shape into balls, and place on a floured surface. Using a rolling pin and more flour as needed to prevent sticking, gently roll out each ball of dough into an 8 inch (20 cm) circle. Use a plate or bowl to help shape the dough into even circles or leave them as is for a more rustic look. Use a soft-bristled brush to brush off any excess flour then use a fork to poke a couple holes in the dough to prevent it from bubbling up while cooking.   →

❖ FOR THE RED BEET FLATBREADS

17½ ounces (500 g) whole red beets

¾ cup (90 g) light rye flour

1 cup (120 g) all-purpose flour

¾ teaspoon salt

¼ teaspoon caraway seeds
(optional)

¼ teaspoon dried thyme (optional)

Cook the lomper: Heat a *takke* to medium-high heat or place a large frying pan directly on the stove over medium-high heat. Put the fan on and open a window if possible. Gently place 1 lompe on the dry, hot takke or pan and cook for about 30 seconds, or until golden brown on the bottom. Flip the lompe and cook for 30 seconds, or until golden brown on the other side.

Place the cooked lompe on a plate and cover completely with plastic wrap, followed by a tea towel to keep the lompe soft and moist. Brush any excess flour from the takke or pan so it doesn't burn. Continue making lomper, using the remaining dough and piling them on top of each other under the plastic wrap and tea towel. The lomper can be served immediately or wrapped and refrigerated for up to 5 days.

Spiced Carrot Streusel Bread

I adore a good carrot cake loaded with warm spices reminiscent of the season. This one is in loaf form and coated with a *smuldre*, or "streusel," topping that's crumbly and irresistible. A bit like *krydderkake*, or "spice cake," it's always a hit and I'm sure you will love it. You can always add in some extra bits, such as chocolate, nuts, and dried fruits, if you're feeling so inclined.

Makes 1 loaf (about 10 slices)

❖ FOR THE BREAD

6 medium carrots, peeled and cut into bite-size pieces

2 cups (240 g) all-purpose flour

1 teaspoon baking soda

1½ teaspoons ground cinnamon

¼ teaspoon ground nutmeg

¼ teaspoon ground cloves

¼ teaspoon ground ginger

½ teaspoon salt

½ cup (100 g) granulated sugar

½ cup plus 2 tablespoons (100 g) dark brown sugar

½ cup (120 ml) canola or vegetable oil

2 large eggs, at room temperature

½ cup (120 ml) whole milk

½ teaspoon vanilla extract

❖ FOR THE STREUSEL

4 tablespoons (56 g) lightly salted butter, melted

6 tablespoons (65 g) dark brown sugar

½ cup (60 g) all-purpose flour

For the bread, in a medium pot, cover the carrots with cold water and bring to a boil. Lower the heat and simmer for 15 to 20 minutes, or until the carrots are tender when pierced with a knife. (Alternatively, steam the carrots for the same amount of time.) Drain the carrots, then transfer to a blender or food processor and purée until smooth. Set aside.

For the streusel, in a medium bowl, combine the melted butter, brown sugar, and flour. Place in the refrigerator while you make the bread.

Preheat the oven to 350°F (180°C). Line a 9 x 5 inch (23 x 13 cm) loaf pan with parchment paper.

In a large bowl, whisk together the flour, baking soda, cinnamon, nutmeg, cloves, ginger, and salt.

In the bowl a stand mixer fitted with the paddle attachment, combine the carrot purée with the granulated sugar, brown sugar, and oil and beat until blended. Add the eggs, 1 at a time, incorporating each egg before adding the next, and beat for 2 to 3 minutes, or until light and creamy. Add the milk and vanilla and beat until blended. Add the flour mixture and beat until just incorporated. Pour the batter into the prepared pan. Break the chilled streusel into pieces with your hands and scatter evenly over the batter. Bake for 1 hour, or until golden brown. Let cool in the loaf pan for 10 minutes, then transfer to a wire rack and let cool completely. Cut into thick slices and serve. Store in an airtight container at room temperature or in the refrigerator for up to 4 days.

Pear and Rutabaga Spiced Loaf Cake

I've become quite smitten with rutabaga since being introduced to the Nordic lifestyle. These large, matte purple, and slightly rough-looking root vegetables, which are a cross between a turnip and a cabbage, are versatile and delicious. They're also referred to as *Nordens appelsin*, or "the North's orange," because of their high levels of vitamin C.

I like to purée the cooked flesh and keep it in the freezer, so I can add it to a variety of recipes throughout the year. Here, I've used it to enhance my spiced loaf cake and thrown in some delightful pears from my neighbor's tree. Not only does it look inviting, but you would also never be able to tell it's made with rutabaga.

If you have larger pears, use a smaller loaf pan and less pears. Store any leftover rutabaga purée for another use.

Makes 1 loaf (about 10 slices)

1 large rutabaga

1 cup (120 g) all-purpose flour

½ cup (60 g) light rye flour

½ cup (100 g) granulated sugar

½ cup (80 g) dark brown sugar

1 teaspoon baking soda

½ teaspoon baking powder

¼ teaspoon ground cinnamon

¼ teaspoon ground nutmeg

¼ teaspoon ground cardamom

½ teaspoon salt

2 large eggs, at room temperature

4 tablespoons (56 g) lightly salted
　butter, melted

¼ cup (60 ml) milk

4 small firm pears

Cut off the top and bottom of the rutabaga, peel the skin with a potato peeler, and cut into small pieces. In a large pot, cover the rutabaga with cold water and bring to a boil. Lower the heat and simmer for 15 to 20 minutes, or until tender when pierced with a knife. Drain the rutabaga, transfer to a blender, and purée until smooth. Let cool.

Preheat the oven to 350°F (180°C). Butter a 9 x 5 inch (23 x 13 cm) loaf pan.

In a large bowl, whisk together the all-purpose flour, rye flour, granulated sugar, brown sugar, baking soda, baking powder, cinnamon, nutmeg, cardamom, and salt.

In a medium bowl, whisk together the eggs, melted butter, milk, and 1 cup (240 ml) of the rutabaga purée. Add this to the flour mixture and stir to combine.

Peel the pears. Cut the bottoms so they stand upright then cut lengthwise in half.

Pour the batter into the prepared pan. Place the pears evenly, stems up, in the batter so they are nearly covered—the batter will rise as the pears cook. Bake for about 45 minutes, or until a toothpick inserted in the center comes out clean. Let cool in the pan for 30 minutes before serving. Keep covered in the refrigerator for up to 4 days.

Outdoor Skillet Bread

When the summer dry spells are long gone and it's once again safe to set up a fire outdoors, we often find ourselves using nature as our kitchen. We cook a variety of things, and this *bålbrød* — "fire bread" — is my go-to, because it can be used for anything. You can eat it with a good drizzle of butter and honey or with a slab of jam on top. For something savory, as soon as this bread feels firm throughout, melt cheese over it then top with meats, fresh herbs, and mixed greens for a pizza-like creation. It's also dreamy dunked into a hearty stew. Let your imagination soar with this one.

Makes 1 skillet bread

¾ cup (180 ml) warm water

1 teaspoon granulated sugar

1 teaspoon (⅛ ounce / 3.5 g) active
dry yeast

1¾ cups (210 g) strong white
bread flour

1 teaspoon salt

1 tablespoon mild-flavored oil

In a jar, combine the warm water, sugar, and yeast and let sit for 5 minutes, or until frothy.

In the bowl of a stand mixer fitted with the dough hook attachment, combine the flour and salt. Add the yeast mixture and the oil and knead on medium-low for about 5 minutes, or until the dough is pliable yet somewhat wet and sticky to the touch. Using a spatula, scrape the dough into a well-oiled large bowl, then cover with a tea towel, and let rise in a warm spot for about 1 hour, or until doubled in size.

Meanwhile, prepare a fire in a tripod or other controlled area with a grill rack set above the flames. The fire is ready when the embers are glowing and there are still a few flames.

Once the dough has doubled in size, place on a lightly floured surface and fold the sides over toward the center to form a ball.

Using a paper towel, spread 1 teaspoon of oil over the bottom of a 9 inch (23 cm) cast-iron skillet. Place the skillet on the grill rack set over the prepared fire. After 1 minute, press the prepared dough into the skillet with a spatula or your fingers, pushing it out to the sides of the pan—be careful not to touch the hot skillet with your hands. Cook the dough for 3 to 5 minutes, or until the bottom of the dough is golden brown and slightly firm. Turn the dough over and cook the other side for about 3 minutes, or until the dough is cooked through. Transfer to a cutting board and let cool slightly. Serve warm. Store leftovers in an airtight bag at room temperature for up to 3 days.

Old Fashioned Tea Cake

Delightfully warm, sweet, and yeasty, this tea cake, with roots in Trøndelag, is somewhere between a fluffy bread and a cake. It could be the Norwegian version of a coffee cake and, though not too sweet, it has a simple sugar and cinnamon topping that makes it the perfect afternoon snack. Serve this right away, while it's still warm, and swoon over it with a big cup of coffee, tea, or cold milk.

Makes about 38 slices

❖ **FOR THE CAKE**

6 cups (720 g) all-purpose flour

¾ cup (150 g) granulated sugar

4 teaspoons (½ ounce / 14 g) instant yeast

½ teaspoon salt

1½ cups (360 ml) lukewarm milk

⅔ cup (150 g) lightly salted butter, melted

2 large eggs, at room temperature

❖ **FOR THE TOPPING**

7 tablespoons (100 g) lightly salted butter, at room temperature

½ cup (100 g) granulated sugar, plus more for finishing

1½ tablespoons ground cinnamon

For the cake, in a large bowl, whisk together the flour, sugar, yeast, and salt. Make a well in the center, add the lukewarm milk, melted butter, and eggs, and mix until well blended and the dough is somewhat wet. Cover with a damp tea towel and let rise in a warm spot for about 1 hour, or until doubled in size.

For the topping, in a medium bowl, blend together the butter and sugar.

Once the dough has doubled in size, preheat the oven to 400°F (200°C). Line a baking sheet with parchment paper.

Place the dough on the prepared baking sheet. With slightly wet hands, spread the dough out to form a rectangular that measures roughly 13 x 11 inches (33 x 28 cm). Poke deep holes throughout the dough with your fingers. Using a spatula, spread the topping over the dough, going all the way to the edges. Sprinkle the cinnamon on top, making a crisscross pattern if desired, and let rise, uncovered, for 30 minutes.

Bake for 18 to 20 minutes, or until the cake is golden brown. Sprinkle 1 to 2 tablespoons of sugar on top, cut into diamond shapes, and serve warm. Keep leftovers at room temperature in an airtight bag for 1 to 2 days.

Tosca Cake

Tosca cake is a Scandinavian favorite, thought to be named after the Italian composer Puccini's opera, *Tosca*, which is based on the French play, *La Tosca*, and premiered in 1900. It had its Swedish premier at the Royal Opera House in Stockholm in 1904 and was referenced frequently in the culture of that time. By the 1930s, recipes for tosca cake started appearing in Swedish cookbooks and it was mentioned in Norwegian newspapers by the 1940s. It's a delicate yet dense sponge cake, encrusted with a caramelized almond topping—the "tosca"—that gives the cake its distinctive character. It's luscious and a true classic that remains as steadfast as the opera that inspired it.

Serves 8 to 10

❖ FOR THE CAKE

3 large eggs, at room temperature

¾ cup (150 g) granulated sugar

½ cup (112 g) lightly salted butter, melted and cooled

¼ cup (60 ml) milk

1¼ cups (150 g) all-purpose flour

1 teaspoon baking powder

❖ FOR THE GLAZE

1 cup (100 g) sliced almonds

½ cup (112 g) lightly salted butter

⅓ cup (65 g) granulated sugar

2 tablespoons milk

2 tablespoons all-purpose flour

For the cake, preheat the oven to 345°F (175 °C). Butter a 9 ½ inch (24 cm) springform cake pan.

In a stand mixer fitted with the whisk attachment, whip the eggs and sugar on medium-high for 5 minutes, or until stiff and light in color. Add the melted butter and milk and whip until blended. Sift the flour and baking powder over the batter and use a spatula to gently fold until just combined. Pour into the prepared pan and bake until golden and mostly set, about 20 minutes.

While the cake is baking, make the glaze: In a large saucepan over low heat, combine the almonds, butter, sugar, milk, and flour and cook, stirring, just until the ingredients are blended and the sugar has dissolved.

Once the cake has baked for 20 minutes, remove it from the oven, and spread the glaze on top. Place the cake back in the oven and bake for 15 to 20 minutes more, or until a toothpick inserted in the center comes out clean. Let the cake cool in the pan before serving. Store in an airtight container at room temperature for up to 3 days.

Caramel and Salted Peanut Swiss Roll

During our first year of living in Norway, we were invited over to a friend's house for a classic Norwegian meal. After dinner, we moved into the drawing room for coffee and cake amidst good conversation. Brought before us was this succulent cake drenched in caramel and decorated with salted peanuts. The name, *svinekamkake*, lovingly translates to "pork loin cake"—perhaps because with some imagination it bears a slight physical resemblance. It was divine. Svinekamkake is the kind of cake that fills you up but leaves you wanting more. The color, the decadence, the richness—everything about this cake reminds me of the season. Serve this after it has sat at room temperature for an hour or so to let the cream and caramel soak into the cake.

Serves 8

❖ **FOR THE CAKE**

4 large eggs, at room temperature

½ cup (100 g) granulated sugar

¾ cup (90 g) all-purpose flour

½ teaspoon baking powder

❖ **FOR THE CARAMEL SAUCE**

2 cups (400 g) granulated sugar

½ cup (112 g) lightly salted butter, at room temperature

1 cup (240 ml) heavy cream

❖ **FOR THE FILLING AND TOPPING**

1¼ cups (300 ml) heavy cream

2 tablespoons confectioners' sugar

Handful of salted peanuts, roughly chopped

For the cake, preheat the oven to 375°F (190°C). Line a 16 x 12 inch (40 x 30 cm) rimmed baking sheet with parchment paper.

In a stand mixer fitted with the whisk attachment, whip the eggs and granulated sugar on medium-high for 5 minutes, or until stiff and light in color. Sift the flour and baking powder over the batter and use a spatula to gently fold until combined. Spread the batter in the prepared baking sheet to form an even rectangle. Bake for 10 to 15 minutes, or until golden brown. While still warm, roll the long side of the cake away from you by gently pushing the cake with one hand and pulling away the parchment paper with other to form a log. Cover with the parchment paper and let cool while rolled up to help the cake keep its shape.

For the caramel sauce, in a heavy-bottomed medium saucepan, heat the granulated sugar over low heat, without stirring but shaking the pan as needed, until melted and golden brown in color. Stir in the butter with a wooden spoon, being careful as it will bubble up. Stir in the heavy cream and simmer for 1 minute, or until well blended. Remove from the heat and let cool slightly.

For the filling, in a large bowl, whip the heavy cream and confectioners' sugar until stiff peaks form.

Gently unroll the cooled cake. Spread the whipped cream all the way o the edges and roll back up again. Arrange the cake, with the seam on the bottom, on a serving tray and pour the warm caramel sauce on top. Sprinkle with the salted peanuts and let sit at room temperature for 1 hour before serving. Keep covered in the refrigerator for up to 3 days.

Forest Roulade

This meringue roulade is an ode to the forest in autumn, when the ground is littered with crunchy white moss (reindeer lichen), wild berry bushes, fallen leaves, stones, and tree logs with cracked bark. It's rich and dark thanks to the chocolate but also light and airy with a touch of crunchy texture from the hazelnuts. There's a subtle taste of juniper in the cream and pops of tartness from the berries. If the forest bed was a cake, this is how I imagine it would be.

Serves 8

4 large egg whites, at room temperature

1 cup plus 2 tablespoons (225 g) granulated sugar

3 tablespoons cocoa powder, sifted

⅓ cup (50 g) chopped toasted hazelnuts, with or without skins

Confectioners' sugar, for dusting

1¼ cups (300 ml) heavy cream

2 tablespoons juniper berries, crushed

Forest berries, such as blueberries, lingonberries, or crowberries, for serving

Preheat the oven to 350°F (180°C). Line a baking sheet with parchment paper.

In a stand mixer fitted with the whisk attachment, whip the egg whites on medium until foamy. Gradually add the granulated sugar, a little at a time, then increase the speed to medium-high, and whip until stiff and glossy peaks form. Transfer two-thirds of the meringue to a bowl and gently fold in the cocoa powder and two-thirds of the toasted hazelnuts until just incorporated. Add the remaining one-third of the meringue to the chocolate meringue and fold just a few times to create a swirl pattern. Spread the meringue on the prepared baking sheet to create a rectangle that measures a 13 x 9 inch (33 x 23 cm) rectangle. Bake for 20 minutes, or until golden brown and set.

Place a piece of parchment paper on the counter and sift some confectioners' sugar on top. Carefully turn out the cooked meringue onto the prepared parchment paper and peel away the parchment it was baked on. Set aside to cool.

Whip the heavy cream and crushed juniper berries together until stiff peaks form.

Spread the whipped cream over the cooled meringue, leaving a ½ inch (1.25 cm) border around the edges and reserving a little whipped cream for the top. Starting on a long side, carefully, roll the meringue around the cream to form a long log. Don't worry if the meringue cracks a little. Place the roulade, seam-side down, on a serving tray. Top with the remaining whipped cream, the remaining hazelnuts, and the forest berries of your choice. Keep covered in the refrigerator for up to 3 days.

Dark Chocolate Beer Cake

As the daylight wanes in the autumn months, an intensely dark chocolate cake is much appreciated, especially a sheet pan cake, which feels like an invitation for others to share in the occasion. I love using beer in my baking to deepen flavors and this cake soaks it all up. You get a decadently rich cake with a soft and fluffy frosting. Keep this cake cold but bring it to room temperature before serving, so the frosting regains its smooth texture and swirls around the fork as you dig in.

Serves 15 to 20

❖ **FOR THE CAKE**

1 cup (240 ml) dark beer, such as a porter or stout

¾ cup plus 2 tablespoons (200 g) lightly salted butter

½ cup (50 g) cocoa powder

2 cups (240 g) all-purpose flour

1⅓ cups (265 g) granulated sugar

1½ teaspoons baking powder

½ teaspoon salt

2 large eggs, at room temperature

⅔ cup (160 ml) sour cream

❖ **FOR THE FROSTING**

3½ ounces (100 g) 70% dark chocolate

⅔ cup (150 g) lightly salted butter, at room temperature

1 cup (120 g) confectioners' sugar

2 tablespoons cocoa powder

3 tablespoons (45 ml) dark beer, such as a porter or stout

For the cake, preheat oven to 350°F (180°C). Butter a 13 x 9 inch (33 x 23 cm) cake pan.

In a small saucepan, warm the beer and butter over low heat until the butter is melted. Whisk in the cocoa powder and set aside to cool.

In a medium bowl, whisk together the flour, granulated sugar, baking powder, and salt.

In a large bowl, beat together the eggs and sour cream. Add the cooled beer mixture and stir to combine. Add the flour mixture and stir until well blended. Pour the batter into the prepared pan. Bake for 30 to 35 minutes, or until a toothpick inserted in the center comes out clean. Cool completely in the pan.

For the frosting, in a small saucepan, bring about 1 inch (2.5 cm) of water to a boil over medium-high heat. Place a heat proof bowl over the saucepan, making sure it doesn't touch the water. Add the chocolate to the bowl, and heat, stirring frequently, until the chocolate is melted. Carefully remove the bowl from the saucepan of water and let the chocolate cool completely.

Once the chocolate is cool, in the bowl of a stand mixer fitted with the paddle attachment, beat the butter, confectioners' sugar, and cocoa powder for 1 minute, or until light and fluffy. Add the cooled chocolate, then slowly pour in the beer and beat until well blended. Spread the frosting over the cake and serve immediately. Keep covered in the refrigerator for up to 4 days.

Ale Griddle Cakes with Buttercream

These griddle cakes will leave you grounded, like a good friend that never lets you down. *Lapper*, like it's counterpart *sveler*, are traditional Norwegian griddle cakes. Here, I've added ale, because dishes infused with beer always seem appropriate in autumn, and because from mythology to home brewing, beer has long held a central place in Nordic culture. These griddle cakes are also an ideal conduit for beer since there are no other strong flavors to contend with. The short cooking time means that most of the integrity of the flavors remains intact. They're fluffy, with sweet and nutty undertones from the beer. A slather of buttercream on top makes them even more luscious.

Makes 10 to 12 griddle cakes

❖ **FOR THE GRIDDLE CAKES**

2 large eggs, at room temperature

⅓ cup (65 g) granulated sugar

½ cup (120 ml) pale ale, brown ale, or wheat beer

1⅓ cups (320 ml) buttermilk

2¼ cups (270 g) all-purpose flour

½ teaspoon baking soda

3 tablespoons lightly salted butter, melted

❖ **FOR THE BUTTERCREAM**

½ cup (112 g) lightly salted butter, at room temperature

⅔ cup (80 g) confectioners' sugar

5 tablespoons (60 g) granulated sugar

For the griddle cakes, in a large bowl, whisk together the eggs and granulated sugar until fluffy. Add the beer and buttermilk and whisk until combined.

In a large bowl, whisk together the flour and baking soda, then add to the batter and stir gently until combined. Whisk in the melted butter. Let stand for 30 minutes—the batter will swell.

Heat a *takke* to medium heat or place a large frying pan directly on the stove over medium heat, and lightly butter. Put the fan on and open a window if possible.

Ladle about ½ cup (120 ml) of batter onto the hot takke or pan to make a griddle cake that measures roughly 6 inches (15 cm) in diameter. Repeat to make more griddle cakes, depending on the size of your takke or pan. Cook for about 2 minutes, or until bubbles appear on the tops of the cakes and the bottoms turn golden brown. Flip the griddle cakes and cook for about 2 minutes more, or until the other side is golden brown. Transfer to a plate and keep warm. Continue making griddle cakes, using the remaining batter and adding more butter to the takke or pan as needed.

For the buttercream, in a small bowl, use a fork to blend the butter, confectioners' sugar, and granulated sugar until combined.

Serve the griddle cakes with the buttercream. Store leftovers covered in the refrigerator for up to 3 days.

Dark
Time

 Mørketid

❖ **THE DAYS SHRINK AND DARKNESS SWELLS** across the land during *mørketiden*, "the dark time." With each new day that draws closer toward the winter solstice, the darkest day of the year, the light slowly fades, becoming something more of a whisper. In the North, the sun's edge doesn't quite rise past the horizon. Yet, in the darkness, nature still sings of the light from the Northern Lights dancing across the limitless sky, illuminating it with vibrant colors. Even the stars' glow and the moon's reflection off the snowy landscape provide some much needed brightness.

While daylight is more precious than ever, the mood is a joyous one and the month of December ushers in the holiday season with sweet cakes, variations of *lefse*, and tables spread with plates of tantalizing cookies. Candles and fireplaces are lit aglow, and lamps are hung in the windowsills. While cold and darkness sweep over the landscape, the warmth of the home and the kitchen keeps everyone in the light.

Dark Chocolate Custard-Filled Doughnuts

As the dark settles in, these doughnuts offer a sweet remedy to what could be a more solemn time of year, as the light fades. While *solboller*, "sun buns" (page 15), celebrate the return of lighter days, *mørketidsboller* celebrate the darkness. These doughnuts, a more recent creation, are found in northern Norway, particularly in Tromsø, where darkness casts its shadow longer than in the south. They're not overly sweet but rather lean into the dark notes, as they should. Dark chocolate covers the fluffy dough and inside is a filling of sweet custard, a reminder that the light is only momentarily hidden.

Makes 15 large doughnuts

❖ **FOR THE DOUGHNUTS**

1¼ cups (300 ml) lukewarm whole milk

2 large eggs, at room temperature

4½ cups (540 g) all-purpose flour

⅓ cup (65 g) granulated sugar

2 teaspoons (¼ ounce / 7 g) instant yeast

1 teaspoon ground cardamom

½ teaspoon salt

6 tablespoons (84 g) lightly salted butter, cubed and chilled

6¼ cups (1.5 liters) canola or vegetable oil, for frying

❖ **FOR THE CUSTARD**

½ cup (100 g) granulated sugar

4 large egg yolks, at room temperature

3 tablespoons cornstarch

480 ml (2 cups) whole milk

½ vanilla bean, split lengthwise, or 1 teaspoon vanilla extract

❖ **FOR THE CHOCOLATE GLAZE**

7 ounces (200 g) 70% dark baking chocolate

⅓ cup (80 ml) heavy cream

For the doughnuts, in a small bowl, whisk together the lukewarm milk and eggs.

In the bowl of a stand mixer fitted with the dough hook attachment, combine the flour, sugar, yeast, cardamom, and salt. Add the milk mixture and knead on low for 10 minutes. Add the butter and knead for about 8 minutes, or until the dough is smooth and very elastic. Transfer the dough to a lightly buttered bowl, cover with a tea towel, and let rise in a warm spot for about 1 hour, or until doubled in size.

For the custard, in a large bowl, whisk together the sugar and egg yolks. Add the cornstarch and whisk until thick and pale yellow. Put the milk in a small saucepan. Scrape the seeds from the vanilla bean into the milk and add the scraped bean. Warm over medium heat until just beginning to simmer then remove from the heat. Remove the vanilla bean, then slowly add the milk to the egg yolk mixture, whisking constantly to avoid curdling the eggs. Pour the mixture back into the saucepan and place over medium heat. Cook, stirring constantly, until thick. Set aside to cool.

Once the dough has doubled in size, place on a lightly floured surface. Using a rolling pin and more flour as needed to prevent sticking, roll out the dough until ½ inch (1.25 cm) thick. Using a 3 inch (7.5 cm) round cookie cutter or the rim of a glass, cut circles out of the dough. Roll out the leftover dough and continue the process until all the dough is used up and you have about 15 circles. Cover the dough with a tea towel and let rise in a warm spot for 30 minutes.

In a large, heavy saucepan, heat the canola or vegetable oil to 350°F (180°C). Line a large plate with paper towels.   →

Carefully lower 3 to 4 doughnuts into the hot oil and fry, turning once, for about 2 minutes per side, or until golden brown on both sides. Transfer to the paper towel-lined plate and let cool. Repeat with the remaining doughnuts.

Fill a piping bag with the cooled custard. Make a hole in the side of each doughnut and pipe the custard into the holes.

For the chocolate glaze, in a small saucepan, heat the chocolate and heavy cream over low heat, stirring until combined. Remove from the heat. Dip the tops of the doughnuts in the chocolate glaze and coat evenly. Set aside for about 10 minutes to allow the chocolate to firm up, then serve right away. These doughnuts will last up to 2 days in an airtight container in the refrigerator.

Thick Lefse with Cinnamon Buttercream

It's been said that *lefse* from the north is light, soft, and tastes like heaven on earth. *Nordlandslefse* is just that. It's a thick and cakey variation of lefse, with a good amount of *smørkrem*—"buttercream"—sandwiched between two layers. It's the kind of treat you'll find served with a cup of dark coffee. It goes by other names, too—*Hardangerlefse, tykklefse,* and *mørlefse*—and can be found throughout the country.

**Makes 4 lefse cakes;
32 individual servings**

❖ FOR THE LEFSE

½ cup (112 g) lightly salted butter

½ cup (120 ml) Norwegian light
   syrup or golden syrup

1 cup (240 ml) buttermilk

½ cup (120 ml) sour cream

¾ cup (150 g) granulated sugar

5 cups (600 g) all-purpose flour

1 teaspoon baking powder

2 teaspoons baking soda

❖ FOR THE BUTTERCREAM

1¼ cups (280 g) lightly salted
   butter, at room temperature

1⅓ cups plus 1 tablespoon (278 g)
   granulated sugar

1 tablespoon ground cinnamon

For the lefse, in a small saucepan, warm the butter and syrup over medium-low heat until combined. Pour the butter mixture into a large bowl. Whisk in the buttermilk, sour cream, and sugar. Add the flour, baking powder, and baking soda and combine to form a smooth dough. Cover and refrigerate for at least 1 hour or overnight.

Place the dough on a well-floured surface. Using a rolling pin and more flour as needed to prevent sticking, roll out the dough until ⅛ inch (3 mm) thick. Use a cake pan or plate, about 8 to 9 inches (20 to 23 cm) in diameter, to cut out 8 large circles.

Heat a *takke* to medium heat or place a frying pan directly on the stove over medium heat. Put the fan on and open a window if possible. Gently place 1 lefse on the dry, hot takke or pan and cook for 2 to 3 minutes, or until golden brown on the bottom. Flip the lefse and cook for 2 to 3 minutes more, or until golden brown on the other side. Transfer the lefse to a wire rack. Continue this process with the remaining dough and stack them on top of each other to cool.

For the buttercream, in a medium bowl, blend together the butter, sugar, and cinnamon.

Take 1 lefse and spread a quarter of the filling on top. Place another lefse on top of the filling. Repeat this process to create four 2-layer lefse cakes. When ready to serve, cut each cake into 8 slices.

Store the lefse cakes in an airtight container in the refrigerator for up to 1 week. Alternatively, wrap the finished lefse, with or without the buttercream, in aluminum foil, place in freezer bags, and freeze for up to 3 months.

Lefse with Creamy Brown Cheese Sauce

Creamy, sweet, and tangy, this type of *lefse* hails from the region of Salten in northern Norway. It's served warm and folded, its contents a dreamy mixture of brown cheese, milk, and sugar that's referred to as *møsbrøm*. Like most traditional dishes, it combines the storable staples of the local people, and was served as a full meal, meant to sustain the community during long hours of physical labor. Today, it's a treat served year-round and regarded with the utmost pride. With its warmth and heaviness, it perfectly suits the winter season and is a dish to fill up on after hours spent in the cold.

Makes 10 møsbrømlefser

❖ FOR THE LEFSE

1 cup (120 g) light rye flour

1 cup (120 g) whole wheat flour

3 cups (360 g) all-purpose flour

1 tablespoon baking powder

2 cups (480 ml) buttermilk

2 tablespoons lightly salted butter, melted

1 tablespoon Norwegian light syrup or golden syrup

❖ FOR THE FILLING

2 tablespoons all-purpose flour

2 cups (480 ml) whole milk

3 tablespoons granulated sugar

8¾ ounces (250 g) brown cheese, grated or sliced

❖ FOR SERVING

Sour cream, lightly salted butter, and Norwegian light syrup or golden syrup

For the lefse, in a large bowl, whisk together the light rye flour, whole wheat flour, all-purpose flour, baking powder, buttermilk, melted butter, and syrup to form a soft dough.

Divide the dough into 10 equal pieces. If using a large frying pan instead of a takke, divide the dough into 20 pieces. Shape each piece into a round and place on a well-floured surface. With a rolling pin and more flour as needed to prevent sticking, roll from the center of the dough to the edges, moving in a circular motion to roll out each round of dough into a very thin circle, about 14 inches (36 cm) in diameter or half that size if using a large frying pan. Using a soft-bristled brush, brush off any excess flour.

Heat a *takke* to medium-high heat or place a large frying pan directly on the stove over medium-high heat. Put the fan on and open a window if possible. Arrange a piece of plastic wrap large enough to cover the lefse in the center of a clean cloth or old sheet large enough to wrap around the lefse.

Gently place 1 lefse on the dry, hot takke or pan and cook for about 30 seconds, or until it begins to bubble on top and turn golden brown on the bottom. Turn the lefse over and cook for about 30 seconds more, or until golden brown on the other side. Place the cooked lefse on top of the plastic wrap and cover with a second piece of plastic. Fold the cloth or sheet over the plastic to keep the lefse soft and moist. Brush any excess flour from the takke or pan, so it doesn't burn. Continue making lefse with the remaining dough. Each time you finish a lefse, open the cloth, remove the top layer of plastic, and place the lefse on top of the others, then cover with the plastic and fold the cloth over.

For the filling, in a large saucepan, whisk the flour with a little of the milk until the flour is fully blended into the milk and place on the stove. Add the rest of the milk and the sugar and bring to a boil over medium-high heat. Add the brown cheese and cook, whisking constantly, for about 5 minutes, or until thickened.

To assemble, warm a lefse on the takke or pan. Spread some filling on top, going all the way to the edges. Place a dollop of sour cream and butter in the middle of the lefse. Fold the lefse in half, then fold in the sides to make an envelope. Repeat to assemble more lefse. Serve warm with syrup.

Thin Lefse with Buttercream

Lefsekling, or rather just *kling*, is a variation of *lefse* that has a strong tradition in the valley of Numedal where we live. It's a soft flatbread that's large, round, and very thin, and is often served with a buttercream filling smothered between two layers. It's no surprise I have a love affair with kling—it's the first lefse I learned to make, and it was also the first one I cooked on a griddle over a wood-fired stove. I hope you love it, too.

**Makes 8 large kling;
64 individual slices**

❖ FOR THE KLING

2 cups (480 ml) whole milk

2 cups (480 ml) heavy cream

¾ cup plus 2 tablespoons (200 g)
  lightly salted butter

8⅓ cups (1 kg) all-purpose flour

2 large egg yolks, at room
  temperature

❖ FOR THE BUTTERCREAM FILLING

2 cups (400 g) granulated sugar

6 cups (1.3 kg) lightly salted butter,
  at room temperature

For the kling, in a medium saucepan, warm the milk, heavy cream, and butter just until the butter has melted. Set aside.

In the bowl of a stand mixer fitted with the dough hook attachment, combine 6 ½ cups (780 g) of the flour and the egg yolks. Add the warm milk mixture and blend until combined. Add the remaining flour, a little at a time, and knead until you get a workable dough.

If using a *takke*, divide the dough into 16 equal portions, about 4 ounces (112 g) each. If using a large nonstick frying pan, divide the dough into 32 equal portions, about 2 ounces (56 g). Cover the dough and refrigerate for 20 minutes.

Place the dough on a well-floured surface. With a rolling pin and more flour as needed to prevent sticking, roll from the center of the dough to the edges, moving in a circular motion to roll out each round of dough into a very thin circle, about 18 inches (45 cm) in diameter if using a takke or the diameter of your large nonstick frying pan. The trick is to get the kling as thin as possible without tearing. If the dough does tear, use your fingers to press it back together. Using a soft-bristled brush, brush off any excess flour.

Heat a takke to medium-high heat or place a large frying pan directly on the stove over medium-high heat. Put the fan on and open a window if possible.

Arrange a piece of plastic wrap large enough to cover the kling in the center of a clean cloth or old sheet large enough to wrap around the kling.

Gently place 1 kling on the dry, hot takke or pan and cook for about 30 seconds, or until it begins to bubble on top and turn golden brown on the bottom. Flip the kling over and cook for about 30 seconds more, or until golden brown on the other side. Place the cooked kling on top of the plastic wrap and cover with a second piece of plastic. Fold the cloth or sheet over the plastic to keep the kling soft and moist. Brush any excess flour from the takke or pan so it doesn't burn. Continue making kling with the remaining dough. Each time you finish a kling, open the cloth, remove the top layer of plastic, and place the kling on top of the others, then cover with the plastic, and fold the cloth over. Let cool completely.   →

For the buttercream filling, in a stand mixer fitted with a paddle attachment, combine the sugar and butter and beat until blended. Evenly spread a good amount of buttercream over a kling and top with a second kling. Repeat with the remaining kling. Cut into 8 large slices (or 4 slices if using a frying pan) and serve immediately or refrigerate for up to 1 week. If freezing, wrap stacks of the filled kling slices in plastic wrap then cover tightly with foil and freeze for up to 6 months, thawing for 30 minutes before serving.

Lefse Rolls

There are sweet variations of *lefse* and there are savory variations. *Lefseruller, or* "lefse rolls," bring both to the party, depending on your filling of choice, and make delightful appetizers. They often feature traditional flavors like smoked salmon with cream cheese and cured meats with salads of beet, egg, or potato. For the lefse, I typically use a potato-based recipe like the soft spelt potato flatbreads in this cookbook (page 73), but any of the soft root vegetable flatbreads (page 176), the lefse from the *møsbrømlefse* (page 212), and the lefse from the *kling fra Numedal* (page 215) will all work as wraps for these. You can fill these with your favorites, but here are some Nordic suggestions that might inspire.

→ *Smoked salmon, cream cheese, arugula, and red onion:* Spread cream cheese evenly across the lefse all the way to the edges. Place smoked salmon in a line, along the center and top with arugula and thin slices of red onion.

→ *Roast beef, remoulade, lettuce, and dill pickles:* Spread remoulade evenly across the lefse all the way to the edges. Place roast beef in a line, along the center. Place lettuce and pickles (halved lengthwise) next to the roast beef.

→ *Pulled pork and red beet salad:* Spread red beet salad evenly across the lefse all the way to the edges. Place pulled pork in a line, along the center.

→ *Pickled Herring, Dijon, sour cream, boiled potatoes, and thinly sliced leeks:* Spread some Dijon and a dollop of sour cream evenly across the lefse all the way to the edges. Place pickled herring in a line, along the center, and top with potatoes and leeks.

→ *Pâté, butter, and pickled red beets:* Spread lightly salted butter evenly across the lefse all the way to the edges. Place thin slices of pâté in a line, along the center, and top with pickled beets.

→ *Brie, walnuts, and black currant jam:* Spread jam evenly across the lefse all the way to the edges. Place brie in a line, along the center, and top with walnuts.

→ *Cured pork and egg salad:* Spread egg salad evenly across the lefse all the way to the edges. Place cured pork in a line, along the center.

Roll the lefse tightly around the fillings to create logs and place on a cutting board with the seam tucked underneath. Cut off the ends of each roll that might not have a lot of filling, then cut the rolls into 2 inch (5 cm) slices, place on a serving tray, and serve.

Other variations: strawberries and sweetened crème fraîche; turkey and Waldorf salad; roasted vegetables and cream cheese; bacon and potato salad; shrimp with lemon mayo; and chicken salad with grapes.

Fat Breads

I reminisce about the scent permeating from a bakery I visited in Gudbrandsdalen that had bakers dancing around, while rolling, flipping, and baking all sorts of traditional delectable goods. Although the bakery is known for many treats, their *fettbrød*, also known as *rumbrød*, stand out. Made with both butter and lard, and flavored with a dash of cardamom, these breads are flaky, indulgent, and sweet. They're rolled thin, so they turn crispy after baking, which gives them a longer shelf life. If you do end up with softer ones, I like to warm them in a dry frying pan the next day and spread some butter on top, followed by a sprinkling of sugar. They're divine this way and it's a lot like how one would serve *småbrød*, a variation on this bread from the same region.

I've omitted the lard, but feel free to include it by replacing half the amount of butter with an equal amount of lard. Plan to start this recipe a day ahead, so the dough can be refrigerated overnight.

Makes about 50 breads

4 cups (480 g) all-purpose flour

¾ cup plus 2 tablespoons (175 g) granulated sugar

1 teaspoon ground cardamom

1½ cups (336 g) lightly salted butter, at room temperature

1 cup (240 ml) whole milk

In a large bowl, whisk together the flour, sugar, and cardamom. Add the butter and use your hands to gently blend until the mixture resembles crumbs. Add the milk and stir with a wooden spoon until the dough comes together. Cover and refrigerate overnight.

Let the dough stand at room temperature for 30 minutes to make it easier to divide and roll out.

Divide the dough into 4 pieces and place on a well-floured surface. Using a rolling pin and more flour as needed to prevent sticking, roll out 1 piece of dough until very thin, about ⅛ inch (3 mm) thick. Using a pastry cutter wheel with rippled edges, cut circles in the dough that measure roughly 4 inches (10 cm) in diameter. Reroll any scraps of dough to make more circles. Continue this process with the remaining pieces of dough.

Heat a large *takke* over medium-high heat or place a large frying pan directly on the stove over medium-high heat. Put the fan on and open a window if possible. Place some fettbrød on the dry, hot takke or pan, and cook for 1 minute, or until golden brown and bubbly on the bottoms. Flip the fettbrød and cook for 1 minute more, or until golden brown on the other sides. Flip again and cook for 15 seconds more to cook out any moisture. Set on a wire rack to cool completely. Continue making fettbrød with the remaining dough. Serve or store in a metal cookie tin for up to 1 month.

Ring Breads

These snail-looking breads are a regional specialty from the area of Mo i Rana. *Rengakaka* have had a strong presence in the local food culture for hundreds of years. The farmers in the area grew barley and, therefore, purists will only use barley flour to make ring breads — although you can omit the barley and use only white flour for a lighter version. Traditionally, these were everyday food, as they could be stored for longer periods of time. Today, they are usually baked for Christmas and Easter. Ring breads take a little time to put together, but they make for a beautiful site on the table, served with butter, cold cuts, and cheese, among other treats.

Makes 16 breads

3¼ cups (390 g) barley flour

1 cup (120 g) all-purpose flour

1 tablespoon baking powder

7 tablespoons (100 g) lightly salted butter, at room temperature

1¾ cups (420 ml) milk

Preheat the oven to 400°F (200°C). Line 2 baking sheets with parchment paper.

In a large bowl, whisk together the barley flour, all-purpose flour, and baking powder. Add the butter and use your hands to gently blend until the mixture resembles crumbs. Add the milk and stir with a wooden spoon until the dough comes together.

Divide the dough into 16 equal pieces. Roll each piece of dough into a long and thin strand that measures about 36 inches (90 cm) in length. Start with one end of a piece of dough and coil it around itself, keeping it flat on the work surface as you go, to form a snail shape with 6 to 7 rings. Don't worry if there is a little space between the rings. Continue this process with the remaining pieces of dough. Arrange the breads on the prepared baking sheets and bake for 20 to 25 minutes, or until golden brown. Let cool before serving. Store in an airtight container at room temperature for a couple of weeks.

Spicy Gingerbread Cookies

The crowning jewel of all holiday cookies has to be *pepperkaker*. With its unmistakable shapes and irresistible flavor, this aromatic and playful treat transcends the cookie tin with some of the most versatile uses for the season—it can be strung up as an advent calendar, used to adorn lit-up trees, featured in stories and tales, and turned into elaborate edible houses and even entire cities. There's just no denying the imprint this cookie has made on the holiday season.

In my opinion, the best pepperkaker hit you with welcoming warm spices in every bite and are strong enough to awaken the senses in the best possible way. You'll find the spices are really pronounced in this version and the dough pliable and easy to work with. I hope they will bring you much joy in the kitchen—both baking and eating.

Makes about 60 to 80 cookies

1⅓ cups (300 g) lightly salted butter

1½ cups (300 g) granulated sugar

1¼ cups (300 ml) Norwegian dark syrup or light molasses

3 teaspoons ground cinnamon

3 teaspoons ground ginger

2 teaspoons ground cloves

1½ teaspoons freshly ground black pepper

2 large eggs, at room temperature

6 cups (720 g) all-purpose flour

1 tablespoon baking soda

In a large saucepan, heat the butter, sugar, and syrup over medium heat until the butter is melted. Add the cinnamon, ginger, cloves, and black pepper and blend. Set aside to cool completely. Once the mixture is completely cool, whisk in the eggs.

In a medium bowl, whisk together the flour and baking soda. Add the flour mixture to the pan with the butter mixture and blend well to form a smooth and relatively firm dough. Transfer the dough to a lightly buttered bowl, cover with plastic wrap, and refrigerate for at least 4 hours and preferably overnight.

Remove the dough from the refrigerator and let stand at room temperature for 15 minutes before rolling out.

Preheat the oven to 350°F (180°C). Line 2 baking sheets with parchment paper.

Place the dough on a lightly floured surface. Using a rolling pin and more flour as needed to prevent sticking, roll out a large piece of the dough until about ⅕ inch (5 mm) thick. The thinner the dough, the crispier the cookies will be. Using cookie cutters, cut the dough into shapes as desired. The dough will become easier to roll out the more it is worked. Arrange the cookies on the prepared baking sheets. Bake, 1 baking sheet at a time, for 8 to 10 minutes, or until golden brown. Set on a wire rack to cool completely. Continue this process with the remaining dough. Serve right away or decorate the cookies with confectioners' sugar or icing. Store in a metal cookie tin for up to 1 month.

Layered Brown Cheese Gingerbread Cake

Pepperkaker is a whimsical dough of make-believe, created in a world of one's own making, where the imagination can dwell and the mouth can feast. It's in this world where I ventured for this cake. I wanted to evoke the magic and sense of *kos*, "coziness," you find in the forest, as you wander through conifer trees, searching for a clearing to settle in under the vast starlit sky.

A spicy and fragrant cake with layers of delicate whipped Norwegian brown cheese caramel frosting is the foundation for the pepperkaker forest nestled above. A *lavvo*, also made with pepperkaker and inspired by the traditional dwelling used by the Sami people, awaits the sojourner with a fireplace nearby. The cookies are made using my pepperkaker recipe (page 226) but hand cut for a rustic look, and dusted with confectioners' sugar to mimic snow. Feel free to decorate as you desire to make this cake magical for you.

Serves 10 to 12

❖ FOR THE BROWN CHEESE CARAMEL SAUCE

1 cup (200 g) granulated sugar

1 cup (240 ml) heavy cream

7 ounces (200 g) Norwegian brown cheese

❖ FOR THE CAKE

1 cup (240 ml) buttermilk

1½ teaspoons baking soda

2½ cups (300 g) all-purpose flour

1½ teaspoons baking powder

2 teaspoons ground cinnamon

2 teaspoons ground ginger

1 teaspoon ground allspice

½ teaspoon ground cloves

½ teaspoon freshly ground black pepper

¾ cup (150 g) granulated sugar

5 tablespoons (50 g) dark brown sugar

1 cup (224 g) lightly salted butter, at room temperature

¼ cup (120 ml) brown cheese caramel sauce

3 large eggs, at room temperature

For the brown cheese caramel sauce, in a small saucepan, bring the granulated sugar, heavy cream, and brown cheese to a simmer. Continue simmering, stirring continuously, for 8 to 10 minutes, or until somewhat thickened. Let cool completely.

For the cake, preheat the oven to 350°F (180°C). Cut pieces of parchment paper so they fit perfectly in the bottom of three 8 inch (20 cm) springform pans. Butter the pans then add the parchment and butter it.

In a medium bowl, whisk together the buttermilk and baking soda and let stand for a couple of minutes.

In a large bowl, whisk together the flour, baking powder, cinnamon, ginger, allspice, cloves, and pepper.

In the bowl of a stand mixer fitted with the paddle attachment, beat the granulated sugar, brown sugar, and butter until light and fluffy. Add the ¼ cup (120 ml) of cooled brown cheese caramel sauce and beat until incorporated. Add the eggs, 1 at a time, incorporating each egg before adding the next. Continue beating for 2 to 3 minutes, or until light and creamy. Add the buttermilk mixture and beat until just blended. Sift the flour mixture over the batter and use a spatula to gently fold until just combined. Divide the batter among the prepared pans. Bake for 20 to 25 minutes, or until golden brown. Let cool for 10 minutes in the pans before removing the parchment paper and transferring the cakes to a wire rack to cool completely. →

❖ FOR THE BROWN CHEESE CARAMEL FROSTING

7 ounces (200 g) cream cheese

1 cup (240 ml) brown cheese caramel sauce

1¼ cups (300 ml) heavy cream

❖ FOR SERVING

Pepperkaker (page 226), dusted with confectioners' sugar

For the brown cheese caramel frosting, in a small bowl, whisk together the cream cheese and the 1 cup (240 ml) of cooled brown cheese caramel sauce.

In a large bowl, whip the heavy cream until stiff peaks form. Add the cream cheese mixture and whip until thick and spreadable.

To assemble, place 1 cake layer on a serving plate or tray and top with a generous amount of frosting, spreading it to the edges of the cake. Arrange the second cake layer on top and repeat the process of adding the frosting, reserving enough frosting to cover the cake. Top with the final cake layer then cover the top and sides of the cake with the remaining frosting, scraping the sides for a "naked" look. Refrigerate the cake for 30 minutes before decorating with pepperkaker and confectioners' sugar. Keep covered in the refrigerator for up to 4 days.

St. Lucia Saffron Buns

St. Lucia Day, *Luciadagen,* falls on December 13, and is celebrated throughout Scandinavia. In Norway, the day is honored with a candle procession in the kindergartens and schools, which is led by one of the children dressed up as St. Lucia, in a white dress with a wreath and candle on their head. The other children follow behind, singing the song "Santa Lucia." As the procession carries forward, the children hand out delicately soft saffron buns called *lussekatter* to symbolize the light. They're shaped in various ways, but the traditional spiral "S" shape is an ancient symbol for the sun and life. Each bun is typically adorned with a raisin or two.

Makes 14 buns

⅔ cup (150 g) lightly salted butter

2 cups (480 ml) milk

4 teaspoons (½ ounce/14 g)
   instant yeast

¼ teaspoon ground saffron or
   saffron threads, gently crushed

¾ cup (150 g) granulated sugar

3 large eggs, at room temperature

7½ cups (900 g) all-purpose flour,
   plus more as needed

1 teaspoon salt

Raisins, for serving

In a medium saucepan, melt the butter over medium heat. Add the milk, yeast, and saffron and whisk until combined. Remove from the heat. Add the sugar and stir to incorporate. Add 2 of the eggs and whisk until combined. Transfer the mixture to a large bowl. Add the flour and salt and mix to form a sticky dough. Turn the dough out onto a lightly floured surface and knead for 5 to 10 minutes or until the dough is smooth and elastic. Cover with a tea towel and let rise in a warm spot for about 45 minutes, or until doubled in size.

Once the dough has doubled in size, preheat the oven to 400°F (200°C). Line 2 baking sheets with parchment paper.

On the same lightly floured surface, divide the dough into 14 equal pieces and roll out each piece into a thick strand. Roll the ends of each strand toward the middle in opposite directions to form an "S" shape. Arrange the buns on the prepared baking sheets, cover with a tea towel, and let rise for 20 minutes.

In a small bowl, whisk the remaining egg. Using a pastry brush, lightly brush the egg on top of the dough. Decorate the buns with raisins. Bake, 1 baking sheet at a time, for 10 to 12 minutes, or until golden brown. Transfer to a wire rack to cool slightly. These buns are best eaten while they are still fresh, on the day they were baked.

Christmas Bread

Julekake, also called *julebrød*, is a sweet bread spiced with cardamom and typically filled with raisins and candied citrus peel. It's a staple on the holiday table and topped with sweet and savory things like butter, brown cheese, white cheese, jams, and smoked cured meats. When the loaves start to dry out, they welcome a good toasting. They also make the most gorgeous bread pudding if you have any slices leftover.

Makes 2 loaves

7 cups (840 g) all-purpose flour

¾ cup (150 g) granulated sugar

4 teaspoons (½ ounce / 14 g) instant yeast

2 teaspoons ground cardamom

2 cups (480 ml) lukewarm milk

2 large eggs, at room temperature

⅔ cup (150 g) lightly salted butter, cut into pieces and chilled

¾ cup (150 g) raisins

¾ cup (100 g) finely diced candied citrus peel

In the bowl of a stand mixer fitted with the dough hook attachment, whisk together the flour, sugar, yeast, and cardamom. Add the lukewarm milk and 1 of the eggs and knead on low for 8 minutes. Add the butter and knead on medium for 5 minutes, or until the dough is very elastic and somewhat moist. Turn the dough out on a lightly floured surface. Knead in the raisins and candied citrus peels. Transfer the dough to a lightly buttered bowl, cover with a tea towel, and let rise in a warm spot for about 45 minutes, or until doubled in size.

Once the dough has doubled in size, preheat the oven to 350°F (180°C). Line a baking sheet with parchment paper.

Divide the dough in half and shape each half into a round. Score the tops of the loaves with a blade. Place the loaves on the prepared baking sheet, cover with a tea towel, and let rise for 30 minutes.

In a small bowl, whisk the remaining egg. Using a pastry brush, lightly brush the egg on top of the dough. Bake for 35 to 40 minutes, or until golden brown. Let cool slightly and serve. Store leftovers in a plastic bag at room temperature for up to 2 days. If you wish to freeze the loaves, place in a freezer bag as soon as they have cooled. To serve, thaw completely at room temperature before warming in the oven for a couple of minutes.

Mother Monsen Cake

This is a rich and buttery cake accented with pops of lemon and a coating of dried currants, almonds, and pearl sugar that adds the most delightful texture. Its appeal lies in how quick it is to pull together and how luxurious the flavors are. It's no wonder it's considered one of the classic Christmas cakes.

The name translates to "Mother Monsen," but the story behind the cake is often lost in the sweetness of it all. Mor Monsen is really Helene Cathrine Büchler, who married Mogens Larsen Monsen, the head of a thriving timber business, who inherited the grand estate of Linderud Gård—*gård* translates to "farm"—which they used more as a playground in the summer months. During these occasions, this cake was often served. The recipe was included in Hanna Winsnes' famous cookbook from 1845, *Lærebog i de forskjellige Grene af Huusholdningen*, with the title of the recipe translated to "Mother Monsen's Visit Cake." You'll find yourself wanting to make this for visitors, too. It's that good.

Serves 15

2 cups (240 g) all-purpose flour

1 teaspoon baking powder

1¼ cups (250 g) granulated sugar

1 cup plus 2 tablespoons (250 g) lightly salted butter, at room temperature

6 large eggs, at room temperature

Zest and juice of 1 small lemon

½ cup (50 g) sliced almonds

¼ cup (35 g) dried currants

1½ tablespoons pearl sugar, plus more for serving

Preheat the oven to 350°F (180°C). Line a 13 x 9 inch (33 x 23 cm) cake pan with parchment paper.

In a medium bowl, whisk together the flour and baking powder.

In the bowl of a stand mixer fitted with paddle attachment, beat the granulated sugar and butter until light and fluffy. Add the eggs, 1 at a time, incorporating each egg before adding the next, and beat for 2 to 3 minutes, or until light and creamy. Add the flour mixture and beat until incorporated. Add the lemon zest and juice and beat just until blended. Pour the batter into the prepared pan. Sprinkle with the almonds, currants, and pearl sugar. Bake for about 25 minutes, or until a toothpick inserted in the center comes out clean and the top of the cake is golden. Sprinkle a little more pearl sugar on top. Cool slightly in the pan before cutting in diagonal shapes and serving. Keep covered in the refrigerator for up to 5 days.

Wafer Cookies

Delicate to the touch, these beautiful cookies will break with the slightest pressure, giving the most delicious crumbs that you are more than welcome to snatch up from the plate.

Not to be confused with *krumkaker*, a similar type of wafer cookie made in the same way, that I included in my first cookbook, these are made with heavy cream or sour cream. They are cooked on a *krumkake* iron embellished with elaborate designs and then rolled into thin cigars to be served during the holiday season. They'll be in great company with ice creams and whipped creams, or whatever else your heart so desires.

Makes about 14 cookies

1 cup (240 ml) heavy cream

½ cup (100 g) granulated sugar

3 tablespoons cold water

¾ cup plus 1 tablespoon plus 1 teaspoon (100 g) all-purpose flour

Butter, for cooking

In a large bowl, whip the heavy cream and sugar together until stiff peaks form. Add the water then sift the flour over the batter and use a spatula to gently fold until just combined. Let stand for 30 minutes.

Place the krumkake iron directly on the stove over medium-high heat or follow the manufacturer's directions if using an electric iron. When the iron is hot, add a little butter at the start to prevent sticking. Depending on the size of your iron, spoon 1 to 2 tablespoons of batter on the iron. Close the iron and cook, flipping once, for about 30 seconds per side, or until light golden. Carefully remove the cookie from the iron and immediately roll it into a cigar shape with your hands. Transfer to a wire rack to cool and repeat with the remaining batter. Store in a metal cookie tin for up to 1 month.

Butter Cookies

These buttery Christmas cookies, a cross between shortbread and sugar cookies, are rich and delicate. Their simple nature disguises their toothsome taste. Each small cookie is topped with almonds that roast ever so slightly as they bake in the oven and a good sprinkling of crunchy pearl sugar. I am particularly drawn to *serinakaker*, and always make a batch or two during the holidays.

Makes 30 cookies

2 cups plus 1 tablespoon (250 g)
   all-purpose flour

2 teaspoons baking powder

⅔ cup (150 g) lightly salted butter,
   at room temperature

½ cup (100 g) granulated sugar

2 teaspoons vanilla extract

1 large egg, lightly beaten,
   plus 1 large egg white, beaten,
   at room temperature

Pearl sugar, for finishing

Sliced or chopped almonds,
   for finishing

Preheat the oven to 375°F (190°C). Line 2 baking sheets with parchment paper.

In the bowl of a stand mixer fitted with the paddle attachment, combine the flour and baking powder. Add the butter and beat until well combined. Add the granulated sugar, vanilla, and the lightly beaten whole egg and beat until well combined.

On a lightly floured surface, roll out the dough into a long log and divide into 30 equal pieces. Roll each piece into a smooth ball, then gently press down on the top of each ball with the back of a fork, creating a faint pattern. Arrange the cookies on the prepared baking sheets. Using a pastry brush, brush the cookies with the beaten egg white and sprinkle with pearl sugar and almonds, using as much or as little as desired. Bake, 1 baking sheet at a time, for 10 to 12 minutes, or until just turning golden. Set on a wire rack to cool completely before serving. Store in a metal cookie tin for up to 1 month.

Brown Syrup Cookies

Brune pinner translates to "brown sticks," which is a direct reference to their appearance but an understatement in terms of their taste. They're similar to *pepperkaker* (page 226) but have a strong burst of syrup and cinnamon and a topping of pearl sugar and almonds to accentuate every bite. Their incredible flavor and how easy they are to make are probably what make them a popular choice when it comes to *syv slags julekaker*, or the "seven kinds of Christmas cookies." I like to use a mixture of white and brown sugar in my recipe for the best flavor and texture. Feel free to swap the almonds for another nut you may prefer or omit them altogether. These cookies will be crunchier towards the ends and a little chewier in the center.

Makes about 60 cookies

2½ cups (300 g) all-purpose flour

2 teaspoons ground cinnamon

1 teaspoon baking soda

½ cup (100 g) granulated sugar

½ cup plus 2 tablespoons (100 g) dark brown sugar

¾ cup plus 2 tablespoons (200 g) lightly salted butter, at room temperature

1 tablespoon Norwegian dark syrup or light molasses

1 large egg yolk, at room temperature, plus 1 large egg, beaten

1 teaspoon vanilla extract

¼ cup (56 g) pearl sugar

1½ tablespoons chopped almonds

Preheat the oven to 350°F (180°C). Line 2 baking sheets with parchment paper.

In a medium bowl, whisk together the flour, cinnamon, and baking soda.

In the bowl of a stand mixer fitted with the paddle attachment, beat the granulated sugar, brown sugar, and butter until light and fluffy. Add the syrup, the egg yolk, and vanilla and beat until light and creamy. Add the flour mixture and beat until combined.

Divide the dough into 6 equal pieces. On a lightly floured surface, roll out each piece of dough into a long and thin rope that measures about 9½ inches (24 cm) in length. Arrange the ropes on the prepared baking sheets, with space in between, then use your fingers to press each rope flat so it's roughly ¼ inch (6 mm) thick. Using a pastry brush, brush the dough with the beaten egg and sprinkle the pearl sugar and chopped almonds on top. Bake, 1 baking sheet at a time, for 10 to 12 minutes, or until golden brown. While still warm, use a knife to cut the flattened ropes, on a diagonal, into small, roughly ½ inch (1.25 cm), strips. Set on a wire rack to cool completely before serving. Store in a metal cookie tin for up to 1 month.

Berlin Wreath Cookies

These traditional Christmas cookies are buttery and sweet, and a little indulgent thanks to the addition of cooked egg yolks. Their soft and flaky interior is complemented by a crunchy pearl sugar exterior, making them one of the most popular holiday cookies. It's thought these cookies originated from a baker in Berlin, before making their way to Norway. This, combined with their wreath shape, explains the reasoning behind the name *berlinerkranser*.

Makes about 50 cookies

2 hard-boiled large egg yolks

2 raw large egg yolks, plus 1 raw large egg white, lightly beaten, at room temperature

⅔ cup (130 g) granulated sugar

1 cup plus 2 tablespoons (250 g) lightly salted butter, at room temperature

2½ cups (300 g) all-purpose flour

Pearl sugar, for finishing

In a small bowl, break down the 2 hard-boiled egg yolks with a fork until smooth and lump free. Add the 2 raw egg yolks and blend together.

In a stand mixer fitted with the whisk attachment, combine the yolk mixture and sugar and whip on medium for a couple of minutes until fluffy and light in color. Change the whisk attachment to the paddle attachment. Add the butter and the flour, a little at a time, and beat until well blended. Cover and refrigerate for 30 minutes.

Preheat the oven to 350°F (180°C). Line 2 baking sheets with parchment paper.

On a lightly floured surface, using your hands, take a small piece of dough and roll into a thin sausage about the same thickness as a little finger and 4 to 5 inches (10 to 12.5 cm) in length. Form the dough sausage into a U shape, then cross 1 end over the other to create a wreath shape with the ends overlapping. Continue this process with the remaining dough.

Arrange the cookies on the prepared baking sheets. Using a pastry brush, lightly brush the cookies with the beaten egg white and sprinkle the tops with pearl sugar. Bake, 1 baking sheet at a time, for 10 minutes, or until light golden. Set on a wire rack to cool completely before serving. Store in a metal cookie tin for up to 1 month.

Syrup Cookies

Sirupsnipper are sweet and spicy Christmas cookies similar in flavor to *pepperkaker* (page 226), but with their own distinct shape, a diamond with fluted edges. Nestled in the center is half of a blanched almond, a bright jewel burrowed in its crown. They're crispy and full of fragrant spices, making them a perfect holiday treat that will last a very long time in the cookie tin—that is, as long as they're not eaten up beforehand!

Makes about 50 cookies

⅓ cup (80 ml) heavy cream

5 tablespoons (75 ml) Norwegian dark syrup or light molasses

⅓ cup (65 g) granulated sugar

4 tablespoons (56 g) lightly salted butter

2 cups (240 g) all-purpose flour

¼ teaspoon baking soda

½ teaspoon ground cinnamon

¼ teaspoon ground cloves

¼ teaspoon ground ginger

⅛ teaspoon freshly ground black pepper

About 25 blanched almonds, halved lengthwise

Line 2 baking sheets with parchment paper.

In a large saucepan, heat the heavy cream, syrup, and sugar over medium heat. Add the butter and stir until the butter has melted. Remove from the heat.

In a medium bowl, whisk together the flour, baking soda, cinnamon, cloves, ginger, and pepper. Add the cream mixture and stir until well blended. Cover and refrigerate for at least 3 hours.

After at least 3 hours, preheat the oven to 350°F (180°C).

Place the dough on a well-floured surface. Using a rolling pin and more flour as needed to prevent sticking, roll out a large piece of the dough until about ⅕ cm (5 mm) thick. Using a fluted pastry wheel or knife, cut the dough on the diagonal to form diamond shapes about 4 inches (10 cm) in length. Arrange the cookies on the prepared baking sheets and gently press an almond half in the center of each cookie. Repeat with the remaining dough. Bake in the center of the oven for 6 to 8 minutes, or until golden brown and cooked through. Store in a metal cookie tin for up to 1 month.

Mulled Wine Doughnuts

Gløgg and *smultringer* are two holiday staples that often share the spotlight—a cup of warm gløgg in one hand and smultringer in the other. Gløgg is Scandinavian mulled wine, served strong and with raisins and almonds tossed in. Smultringer are fried cake doughnuts and considered one of the seven traditional types of Norwegian Christmas cookies. It made sense then that these two should come together to form one glorious treat.

Makes about 12 doughnuts

❖ **FOR THE DOUGHNUTS**

1 large egg, at room temperature

6 tablespoons (75 g) granulated sugar

1½ cups (180 g) sifted all-purpose flour

1 teaspoon baking soda

¾ teaspoon ground cardamom

¼ cup (60 ml) heavy cream

¼ cup plus 2 tablespoons (90 ml) sour cream

4¼ cups (1 liter) canola or vegetable oil, for frying

❖ **FOR THE GLAZE**

1 cup (240 ml) red wine, plus more as needed

1 tablespoon granulated sugar

2 slices orange peel, pith removed

1 slice fresh ginger

1 cinnamon stick

1 star anise

½ teaspoon allspice pods

1 cup (120 g) confectioners' sugar, plus more as needed

❖ **FOR SERVING**

½ cup (60 g) almonds, finely chopped

½ cup (75 g) raisins, finely chopped

For the doughnuts, in a medium bowl, whisk together the egg and granulated sugar for 5 minutes, or until light and fluffy.

In a separate medium bowl, whisk together the flour, baking soda, and cardamom.

In the bowl of a stand mixer fitted with the whisk attachment, whip together the heavy cream and sour cream until stiff peaks form. Fold in the egg mixture and stir until combined. Add the flour mixture and stir until the flour is incorporated and the dough is a little sticky and stiff. Cover the bowl with plastic wrap and refrigerate overnight.

Place a wire rack on top of a stack of paper towels and place it near the stove.

In a large heavy-bottomed pot, heat the canola or vegetable oil over medium-high heat until it reaches 320°F (160°C).

While the oil is heating up, place the dough on a lightly floured surface. Using a rolling pin and more flour as needed to prevent sticking, roll out the dough until about ⅖ inch (10 mm) thick. Using a doughnut cutter or 2 graduated round cookie cutters, cut out about 12 doughnuts.

When the oil is hot, carefully lower a few doughnuts into it, leaving space between them, and cook for 30 seconds, or until the bottoms have turned golden brown. Flip the doughnuts over with a wooden skewer and cook for 30 seconds more, or until golden brown on the other side. Transfer to the wire rack set over paper towels. Continue with the remaining dough. Let the doughnuts cool completely.

For the glaze, in a medium saucepan, bring the wine, granulated sugar, orange peels, fresh ginger, cinnamon stick, star anise, and allspice to a boil. Lower the heat and simmer, stirring frequently, for 10 to 15 minutes, or until reduced to ¼ cup (60 ml) and no less. Remove and discard the orange peel, ginger, and whole spices.

In a wide bowl, whisk together the confections' sugar and the mulled wine mixture until smooth and somewhat thick. If the glaze is too thick, add a little more wine or water, and if it's too thin, add a little more confectioners' sugar. You want the glaze to sit well on top of the doughnuts and not run down the sides. Dip the tops of each doughnut in the glaze, moving the doughnuts as needed to cover the tops. Sprinkle the tops with the almonds and raisins before the glaze sets. Store in an airtight container at room temperature for up to 2 days.

Index

Acknowledgements

❖

There are never enough words to express my love and gratitude for my husband, Espen, and my son, Oliver—my companions in life. Thank you for your endless support and for joining me in countless food adventures. Gathering wild edibles, cooking over open fires, afternoon teas, trips to the café, random baking sessions, and just creating with you brings me the upmost pleasure. Most of all, thank you for teaching me how much better food is when it's experienced and shared with the ones you love.

I also wish to thank my wonderful family, near and far, for always encouraging me. Each of you play a role that continues to shape my journey in the most wonderful way. I love you all. Dad and Mom, I'm especially grateful for all you do.

I want to thank my community and friends, who welcome me in with open arms, provide me with ingredients from their gardens, and gather with me to share in meals of celebration.

To all the Norwegian bakers, home cooks, producers, farmers, chefs, and food lovers I have met, who have shared their expertise, their passion, and their baked goods with me, thank you. I'm inspired by you daily. You carry the traditions of this land, and you also create and innovate, adding more depth and richness to our food culture. Thank you for your hard work, and for feeding and nourishing us.

I wish to thank my editor, Julie Kiefer, for believing in this book and for the opportunity to share my love of Norwegian food culture again. To the entire Prestel team for their hard work in bringing this book to life.

Finally, thank you, dear reader, for joining me on this journey to bake more mindfully with each new season.

About the Author

Nevada Berg is the author and creator of the award-winning Norwegian food and culture website, *North Wild Kitchen*. Her recipes and stories are inspired by tradition and history, as well as innovative approaches to Norwegian ingredients. In 2018, Nevada released her first cookbook internationally with resounding success— it was named one of the best cookbooks for the fall by *The New York Times*. Her work has appeared in various national and international print and online media. She was also the TV program leader for the Scandinavian Food Channel's "Cheese Journey" series. Nevada is regarded internationally as one of the most recognized voices for Norwegian food. She resides in the Medieval Valley of Numedal with her Norwegian husband and son.

www.northwildkitchen.com

© Nevada Berg 2023

Prestel Verlag, Munich · London · New York
A member of Penguin Random House Verlagsgruppe GmbH
Neumarkter Strasse 28 · 81673 Munich

Library of Congress Control Number is available; a CIP catalogue
record for this book is available from the British Library.

The author has received support from The Norwegian Non-Fiction
Writers and Translators Association.

Editorial direction: Julie Kiefer
Copyediting: Lauren Salkeld
Design and layout: kral & kral design
Production management: Cilly Klotz
Separations: Helio Repro, Munich
Printing and binding: Livonia Print, Riga

Penguin Random House Verlagsgruppe FSC® N001967

Printed in Latvia

ISBN 978-3-7913-8861-8

www.prestel.com